Stress-Free Potty Training

Second Edition

Stress-Free Potty Training

A Commonsense Guide to Finding the Right Approach for Your Child

Second Edition

Sara Au

Peter L. Stavinoha, Ph.D.

AMACOM

American Management Association

New York • Atlanta • Brussels • Chicago • Mexico City
San Francisco • Shanghai • Tokyo • Toronto • Washington, D.C.

This publication is designed to provide accurate and authoritative information in regard to the subject matter covered. It is sold with the understanding that the publisher is not engaged in rendering legal, accounting, or other professional service. If legal advice or other expert assistance is required, the services of a competent professional person should be sought.

Library of Congress Cataloging-in-Publication Data

Au, Sara.
  Stress-free potty training : a commonsense guide to finding the right approach for your child / Sara Au and Peter L. Stavinoha.
    pages cm
  Earlier edition: 2008.
  Includes bibliographical references and index.
  ISBN 978-0-8144-3666-0 (pbk.) — ISBN 978-0-8144-3667-7 (ebook) 1. Toilet training. 2. Child rearing. I. Stavinoha, Peter L. II. Title.
  HQ770.5.A9 2016
  649'.62—dc23   2015007771

Illustrations by Kelly Light.

About AMA

American Management Association (www.amanet.org) is a world leader in talent development, advancing the skills of individuals to drive business success. Our mission is to support the goals of individuals and organizations through a complete range of products and services, including classroom and virtual seminars, webcasts, webinars, podcasts, conferences, corporate and government solutions, business books, and research. AMA's approach to improving performance combines experiential learning—learning through doing—with opportunities for ongoing professional growth at every step of one's career journey.

Printing number

10 9 8 7 6 5 4 3 2 1

Contents

Introduction
and Philosophy

Parenting is all about teaching your children everything you can to help them become functioning members of society. From the moment they are born, every single act we do teaches them something, for better or worse. As babies, when they cry, we give them food. When they are tired, we rock them to sleep. When they pee and poop, we change their diaper.

Hmmmm . . . let's think about that last one again. Until this point in their very short lives, they have learned that the correct thing to do is to eliminate waste into a diaper. We've taught them this lesson, and most of us have probably taught it well. Your children are so good at this skill, they probably don't even think about it anymore.

That's all about to change.

Potty training encompasses not only teaching new skills to your child, but also unlearning behaviors they thought they already had down pat. There's no getting around it. Potty training is a huge undertaking for both kids and parents alike. Going into a diaper has become second nature to your kids, just as using a toilet is second nature to adults. Imagine if someone came to you one day and said you couldn't use a toilet any-more, that you had to use this newfangled thing that was nearly as big as you are and made loud, scary noises! You'd probably be a little confused and intimidated.

Does this perspective give you some idea of what your child is about to experience? Good! That's what this book is all about: Helping parents view things from a child's point of view. Potty training should be stress free for parents, and (as much as possible) for kids, too! Stressing about this major milestone will only harm the process, bog it down, and eventually, derail it. So, in keeping it stress free, you are doing what's best for your son or daughter.

You—being the conscientious parent that you are—want to go about potty training in a careful, thoughtful way that considers your child's in-dividual needs. You know this is a big step and you want to make it as easy and comfortable for your "baby" as possible. You've probably heard horror stories from other parents and want to avoid getting into those kinds of situations yourself. In short, you want to do right by your child.

Our Philosophy

Our methods are not tricks we guarantee will work in a prescribed amount of time. Nor do we give you step-by-step directions that if fol-lowed result in absolute certain success. Parents do not control this pro-cess, nor do we really control any process with our children. That might sound shocking, but get used to the idea that you are not really in charge here. Our philosophy is that as parents we can manage and influence the training, but that children themselves control it. They have their own nat-ural pace at which they will learn to use the toilet. Through thoughtful planning and effective communication with your unique child, you are setting the stage for your child to own the process and be successful at it.

If you're like many parents, you may feel overwhelmed at the thought of starting to potty train. Unlike riding a bike, you probably have no memories of learning bathroom skills as a child, so how can you teach them to your son or daughter? To boot, others (maybe your mother- or sister-in-law, or that oh-so-helpful neighbor . . .) are often watching over your shoulder, which can leave you anxious and unsure in your abilities to handle this fundamental parenting task.

You're not sure about the hype of those train-in-one-day programs, but on the other hand, can't imagine doing nothing until your child decides to do training on his own. After all, he has no trouble walking around in a wet or dirty diaper for hours. What all this tells you is that you can't start by planning on the exact amount of time it is going to take to train! (Talk about setting yourself up for failure.) Every child potty trains differently; besides, even those one-day methods take a great many more days in preparation.

We believe toileting proficiency is one of the most important skills you'll teach your child, fundamental to personal hygiene, health, and even social relationships for the rest of his/her life. Being comfortable with one's own body starts with this first foray into being responsible for oneself. So, you don't want to rush in headlong without a thoughtful plan. We recognize, of course, that you don't want to dilly dally either. You want to instruct your child in the most insightful, caring way possible, and to do that you must take his or her individual personality into account.

But where to begin? You don't want to miss your window of opportunity with your toddler, but you don't want to force the issue too early and short circuit the whole process either.

Welcome to the real world of parenting, where there's no magical solution to any tough issue, just advice from experts and veteran parents, a multitude of proven strategies and tons of moral support, and of course, your own instincts and knowledge of your child—the most important ingredient.

In fact, you already have the knowledge you need to help your toddler potty train; you just may need to be pointed in the right direction. You know your child best. You know everything about him. You know his likes and dislikes, what motivates him most, and the signs he's reached his breaking point. For example:

➤ You know if you get him up and out the door before 9 a.m. he'll be in a great mood all morning, but if you dally and miss the window of opportunity, he'll become cranky an hour before his regular naptime.

➤ You know it takes her a good 15 minutes to warm up to anyone besides you and your spouse, even her beloved grandparents.

➤ You know how to say "no" in many different ways, because if you just came out and said it flatly, he'd double his efforts to do whatever is off limits.

➤ You know she'll be climbing on top of your childless friend's brand-new glass coffee table before your visit is over.

➤ You know he'll copy anything his 5-year-old cousin does.

You already know this and much more about your child. You're the expert. Believe it or not, these are the keys to unlock that potty-training door.

Our Approach

What *Stress-Free Potty Training* does is channel that knowledge and help you figure out what kind of approach will work best. Dr. Pete Stavinoha, a dad and pediatric neuropsychologist, will give you a peek inside your child's mind and help you potty train based on his or her individual personality. Sara Au, a mom and parenting writer, has culled together experiences from other parents across the country who are either in the midst of or have recently finished potty training their children.

We know your child is unique, special, and already has his or her own individual personality. The kinds of attempts that may have worked for your sister (or sister-in-law!), your neighbors, or your friends, make you shake your head in defeat because you know those things won't work for your child. And you know what? You're probably right! Children don't all respond alike, especially when it comes to something as personal as potty training. What prods one child in the direction of the bathroom could just as often cause another to run screaming in the other direction.

Child psychiatrists Drs. Stella Chess and Alexander Thomas are frequently credited with bringing to bear modern views of temperament in children. Over the past fifty years, researchers have identified a number of characteristics that describe how children interact with the people and world around them. Whereas scientists are not in complete agreement about what to call the individual traits that make up temperament, developmental psychologists tend to agree that temperament consists of a group of brain-based, inborn characteristics that guide a person's reaction to the world and provide a basis for the development of personality. So, two children with two different temperaments may respond very differently in the very same situation—each is responding to stimuli in part according to their unique temperament.

In digesting the science of temperament for this book, we have grounded our temperament types according to several common traits identified by researchers over the years. We've tried to break these down into commonsense temperament types that every parent will be able to recognize. Dr. Pete created five typical categories—Goal-Oriented, Sensory-Oriented, Internalizing, Impulsive, and Strong-Willed—and advises specific ways your child will best receive potty-training lessons. Keep in mind, most people have characteristics of a number of temperaments, so don't be surprised if your child shows strong elements of two or even three temperament types. This is actually pretty common and, in fact, helpful because it will mean you will have more strategies at your disposal.

We start with a short quiz to help you figure out where you are with your child and your particular situation. We've left lots of room for your notes in this section, as potty training is a very fluid (no pun intended) process. Next, we outline a number of Universal Strategies you can implement and steps you can take regardless of your child's personality. Some of these are very subtle changes; many involve changing your own behavior.

From there, we take you through the five different personality types and help you determine where to start with your child. Please remember, however, that these personality types are generalizations, and your child may not fall squarely in one camp or another. It may be that he or she exhibits the hallmarks of more than one type. Or, you may even see some other personality traits, latent until now, come to the surface during this profound change of life. For example, a child who is normally very laid back might decide to exercise her right to keep tight control over her own

STRESS-FREE POTTY TRAINING

bodily functions when you try to potty train her. Often, this would be a sign she's not ready to toilet train, but sometimes it stems from an underlying strong will that as yet hadn't had a reason to show itself. In this case, while you'd originally have placed her in the Goal-Directed category, you'd now want to place her in the Strong-Willed category, and the approaches to potty training vary a great deal between the two. Since we know you are the expert here, we leave it up to you to decide which steps may resonate more fully with your individual child. We'd like you to read through the entire book before making a decision of how to begin.

After reading this book, many of you may set about potty training in a very different way than you'd ever have expected. Some of you may have to double back and reassess the category or categories into which your child falls. But all of you will gain some insight into your child's mindset.

Throughout this book, segments called "Potty Talk" will offer ideas for specific dialogues to use with your child. We provide these because a parent's words, tone, and attitude convey strong messages to a child in training These suggested dialogues are just that—suggestions. Use them if you like them, change them to fit your own children—both in terms of their age and understanding of words—and make them fit your own situation. These dialogue examples should just get you started.

What's New in the Second Edition

Stress-Free Potty Training was first published in 2008 and became an immediate success. It has now sold more than 35,000 copies. While the act of potty training a child hasn't changed over the years, many new approaches to it are being taken today. This revised, updated, and expanded Second Edition reflects these approaches and adds concepts and information that our readers have told us they would like to see.

For example, one of the most common questions from parents was about children who show lots of interest in potty training early, only to lose interest the moment the parent becomes invested in the process. In response, Chapter 2 includes a new section on this frustrating problem. In

Chapter 3, you will find new material on using apps and websites to help in training your child. This section also includes a discussion of the dangers of disseminating potty-training photos and videos through social media.

Major changes to this edition are also reflected in a reorganization and update of Chapter 3, "Apply Universal Strategies," with four new approaches offered: keeping perspective, communicating clearly, giving good directions, and acting like a coach. Further, Chapter 9 has been renamed and completely overhauled, now dealing with the various types of interruptions to potty training—illness, vacation, moving, a new baby, divorce—that can negatively affect a child, and offering tips on how to handle these issues.

A completely new Chapter 10, "Overcoming Challenges and Obstacles," has been added to this edition as well. The chapter examines some of the most common types of problems parents and children face, such as refusal, withholding, and delays in skill acquisition—that can negatively impact the child and family. An especially insidious hurdle explored in this discussion is constipation, as Dr. Pete takes you through its psychological, as well as possible medical causes, and ways you can help your child overcome them. Finally, the chapter includes information about sensory issues that can complicate the way children learn how to go on the toilet.

A Few Important Notes

No one can force another human being to eat, sleep, or go to the bathroom. If your child offers fierce resistance to any of our suggested tactics, back off immediately. You may need to reevaluate his or her readiness, personality type, or any outside concerns. Or perhaps you'll just need to try another of our suggested approaches. Remember, your role is to influence and manage potty training, but you cannot control it.

To avoid sounding repetitive or wordy, we switch up our pronoun use from sentence to sentence, paragraph to paragraph. In the sections where we discuss information specific to boys or girls, we'll clearly spell that out for you.

There are an infinite number of factors affecting your child's interest, or non-interest, in toileting. (For example, one child was so set on imitating his dad peeing into a urinal that his mom had to first break him of the urge to spray the bathroom wall before she could get him to pee into the toilet.) We attempt to address as many as possible in this book, but by no means have we imagined every possible scenario. Take the advice in this book as a guideline, use what you like, and leave what you don't.

Relax, you are potty training the stress-free way! We promise your child will not go off to college in diapers. She or he will learn how to go to the bathroom in a socially acceptable way. With careful, thoughtful help from you—the most important person in his/her life—they will get through this transitional period of life with flying colors!

Let's get started!

1

Identifying Your Child's Personality Type

In order to identify the most dominant characteristics of your child's personality, we've created a short quiz for you based on common behaviors. You already know what makes your child tick, and taking this quiz will help you channel that knowledge into the science of psychology, and from there into the best ways to potty train. By exploring kids' reactions to people and their environment, we can loosely separate them into groups with similar reactions.

In reading through the quiz, you may feel a great deal of the statements are negative in nature. You are correct. It's unfortunate, but much of what differentiates one type of personality from another is the stimuli that cause negative reactions. For this to seriously be useful for your family, you must answer truthfully, even if you don't like what that says about your child. We know your children are adorable, unique, sweet, loving kids. But as wonderful as every child is, there is no way around some of the negative-sounding aspects needed to categorize them for the purposes of this book. Grouping them is what will help you determine the best way to begin potty training. Don't worry that this means the personality types themselves are negative. They are not.

So before you jump into the meat of the book, go through this short quiz and rank each of the statements in order of how often they describe your child's conduct. Add up the scores and the highest number will show your child's most dominant trait or traits.

Each parent should take this quiz separately and you can then compare answers. Because each child at any given moment responds to whatever set of stimuli is in front of them, they may display character traits to Mom differently than to Dad. Evaluating any overlap or difference of opinion is a terrific way to create a thoughtful, planned approach to potty training. And remember, it is perfectly normal for many children to fall into two, sometimes even three, different groups, and in these cases you should combine the advice in each of those chapters.

After the personality quiz for your child, there is a series of thought-provoking parenting questions we urge you to consider about yourself before beginning to toilet train. These will give you clues into your own temperament and also help you frame your potty-training techniques.

Quiz

Rate the following statements according to how true they are about your child. Once finished, add up the total points for each group. A score of 24 or above indicates a dominant trait or traits, although secondary or tertiary traits with a score of 22–23 should be kept in the back of your mind.

Rating Scale

1 = This is rarely or never true about my child.
2 = This is sometimes true about my child.
3 = This is often true about my child.
4 = This is nearly always true about my child.

GROUP A

➤ My child is bothered by tags in clothes, hates elastic waistbands, and is irritated by certain fabrics. _____
➤ My child startles a great deal at loud noises like the vacuum cleaner, lawn equipment, or even a door slamming. _____
➤ My child seems overstimulated in crowds to the point that we simply don't take him/her out to big events much at all. _____
➤ My child seems to refuse certain foods based on texture or smell. _____
➤ My child has an intense reaction when her/his hands are dirty or wet. _____
➤ If I don't get the bathwater temperature just right, my child strongly resists getting into the tub. _____

➤ As a parent, I am always worried about my child's comfort because she/he falls apart when she/he is the least bit uncomfortable. _____

➤ My child backs away from attempts at physical affection like hugs and kisses from anyone outside our immediate family. _____

Total _____

GROUP B

➤ My child just doesn't get into things the way other kids do; baby-proofing the house was almost unnecessary. _____

➤ My child clings to me more than my friends' kids of the same age seem to do, and gets intensely upset if I try to leave him/her alone for a moment with someone else like a babysitter or even Grandma. _____

➤ When we go places or meet friends out, my child seems to get even more clingy and shy. I don't think this is simply the stranger anxiety that is common in babies because these are people we see frequently enough for him/her to know them. _____

➤ My child seems afraid of lots of things (even imagining complex fears that seem to come from nowhere), and this is especially true at bedtime. _____

➤ My child seems unsure of him/herself in any new situation. It takes him/her a really long time to warm up and get comfortable. _____

➤ Rather than jump into a new activity, my child likes to watch for a long time. She/he also needs some prodding to join in with the group. _____

➤ If I say "no" to my child or set a limit, he/she immediately becomes upset and seems to retreat into him or herself. _____

➤ Once my child is upset, she/he can't seem to move beyond it for a while. She/he stays sad or pouts for a really long time. _____

Total _____

GROUP C

➤ My child usually sticks with an activity for a while before she/he moves on to the next activity. _____

➤ My child isn't distracted easily from a task and likes to finish things once she/he has started. _____

➤ My child really enjoys when she/he has something tangible at the end of a project (like a painting, drawing, or stack of blocks). _____

➤ My child is usually good about following directions. _____

➤ My child asks questions about how to do something, and asks for help when she/he needs it. _____

➤ My child does not ask me to do things for him/her; is fine doing things independently. _____

➤ My child doesn't refuse my offer to help though, and likes it when we work together on a project. _____

➤ My child likes to show me what he/she has done after finishing something and seems to take real pride in his/her accomplishment. _____

Total _____

GROUP D

➤ My child really likes to be independent, and he/she is very resistant to anyone helping him/her. In fact, if I try to help, he/she usually gets mad at me. _____

➤ My child can be very stubborn. If something is her/his idea, she/he really works hard. If it is my idea, there is almost nothing I can do to get her/him to do it. _____

➤ My child has no problem telling me "no," and she/he can be defiant and resistant. _____

➤ My child tends to get angry quickly, and when she/he is angry it seems like the emotion is really intense. _____

➤ When I set a limit or say "no" to my child, she/he gets angry and tantrums or broods for a long time after. _____

➤ My child's tantrums can last for more than 15 or even 30 minutes at a time, and there is little that I can do to shorten them. _____

➤ When I try to finesse my child into doing something she/he does not want to do by prompting or cajoling, the more vocal and louder my child gets in resisting me. _____

➤ My child seems resistant to most attempts at discipline/time-out. Instead of just doing the time-out, she/he constantly fights it and won't stay in time-out. _____

Total _____

GROUP E

➤ My child has a hard time staying with any activity for more than a few moments. Even if she/he is doing something she/he enjoys, she/he seems to get distracted to something else very easily. _____

➤ My child is extremely impatient and can never wait her/his turn for something. _____

➤ My child seems to enjoy lots of stimulation—she/he likes it when there are lots of people around and lots of things going on. _____

➤ My child is very active and loves to climb. I have to watch him/her really carefully because before I know it she/he is on top of the couch, on the table, or in some other dangerous place. _____

➤ My child has a really hard time staying in one place or staying still. She/he hates being in a highchair, and she/he rarely stays seated long enough to do things like draw or color or build. _____

➤ My child is gung-ho to try new physical activities, and she/he is usually quick to try out all the equipment on the playground (even the larger equipment designed for bigger kids). _____

➤ I have a hard time keeping up with my child at the store or in the mall. He/she is always on the move, and he/she likes to have me chase him/her around in a game of cat-and-mouse. _____

➤ My child makes friends with practically everyone and does not seem shy around new people; he/she is often described as a "social butterfly." _____

Total _____

    Group A = Sensory-Oriented Child
    Group B = Internalizing Child
    Group C = Goal-Directed Child
    Group D = Strong-Willed Child
    Group E = Impulsive Child

Summary of Personalities

Sensory-Oriented Child   These are children who have intense reactions to the otherwise normal sensory stimuli of touch, sounds, smells, and tastes. For example, they are often extremely picky eaters, can't stand loud crowds, and incessantly itch at things like tags in the backs of shirts. They may overreact emotionally, and are routinely anxious, shy, and cautious. They are slow to try anything new. When well within their comfort zone, they are usually very easygoing. But they have a tendency to overfocus on anything that might cause them discomfort, and when those sensory issues take over, it can be difficult to calm them down.

Internalizing Child   Serious and conservative, these children often spend a great deal of time and energy considering a situation, weighing their options, before they act. They will practice a new activity or skill in their heads before making an attempt at it; they want to be able to do it perfectly. These children are easily frustrated if success does not come to them quickly, and this tends to inhibit their risk-taking and exploration. If you've never felt the need to baby-proof your house, you probably have an Internalizer. Their fears can be provoked easily, and so they have the inclination to withdraw from new things. These children prefer to be in close proximity with a parent, and they very much enjoy being held.

Goal-Directed Child   These children are generally logical, reasonable, and willing to follow your directions or suggestions. If you are excited about things, they are too. These children are curious and seek knowledge. They are adaptable and tend to go with the flow, but once they focus in on a goal they persist and see it through. These kids are hardwired to enjoy accomplishment. Their mood is generally positive, and they tend to be mild to moderate in terms of activity level. When faced with new situations, they will strike a balance between curiosity and caution. If upset, they can get over it relatively quickly and easily. Although every child has an occasional tantrum, it doesn't happen on a regular basis with a Goal-Directed Child.

Strong-Willed Child   Often described as stubborn, these children tend to have strong, somewhat negative, reactions. They are slow to adapt to new things that are not of their choosing or of their discovery. When they feel like they are in control, they can be relatively easy to get along with. However, when they feel they're being manipulated or forced into something, they are quick to perceive and resist it. Strong-Willed Kids can often be unpredictable in behavior and emotions, at times making their parents feel like they are always two steps behind. They may be rather moody and quickly engage in temper tantrums that are more intense and lengthy than those of other children.

Impulsive Child   If you've ever likened your child to Curious George®, he or she is probably Impulsive. These kids are energetic and extremely active. Typically risk takers, they are the ones who climb all of the furniture and go out of their way to find new physical (read: dangerous) activities. In other words, they're the first to go down the big-kid slide at the park, have no fear when jumping into the swimming pool for the first time, have no fear of climbing, etc. Although reasonably directable, they don't like to be bored and frequently seek out new ways to stimulate themselves much to parents' chagrin. Although outwardly friendly and garrulous, Impulsive Kids also tend to be easily distracted and have trouble persisting in an activity. Tantrums are often strong but over quickly.

Parents' Notes

Now that you've had an opportunity to examine your child's personality traits, before you make your plan, you also need to think about your own first responses to common potty-training situations. Step up to the mirror and honestly write down the first answer that comes to your mind. There is no one right or wrong answer. It's all very subjective—knowing yourself is almost as important as knowing your child when you begin something this emotionally charged. Have your spouse do the same, separately. Make sure your expectations are realistic and that both of you are prepared for the variety of messes that come with potty training. Use the blank pages at the end of the chapter to record notes from this conversation, and refer back to them as you read the rest of the book.

➤ I need/want to potty train my child because . . .

➤ I need/want my child to be successfully in underwear by (date) because . . .

➤ I need/want my child to be dry at night by (date) because . . .

➤ If we don't make either of these dates, I'll feel . . .

➤ If my child wet herself in the middle of the grocery store I would . . .

➤ If my child had an accident on the living-room rug, I would . . .

➤ If my child were to smear feces on the bedroom wall in the middle of the night, I would . . .

➤ If I was at a friend's house with my child and she had an accident on their living room rug, the first thing I would do is . . .

➤ The thought of being on a long car ride with a child who is potty training scares me because . . .

➤ If my child, in the middle of a crowded restaurant, loudly announces he has to "poop real bad," I would . . .

➤ I will wait (x # days) before taking my newly potty-trained child anywhere in underwear because . . .

➤ If my naked child couldn't quite make it to the bathroom and I could see the poop was coming out, I would . . .

➤ If my child soiled himself with feces in a public place, I would . . .

➤ If my child takes a year to potty train I will feel . . .

➤ I'm really stressing out about potty training because . . .

Now, reflect on your answers and talk them over with your partner. After you read the book through, come back to this page and contemplate your answers again. Take your thoughts on all of the above scenarios and put them into the context of what you've learned from this book about your child and their personality types. If you have specific dates by which your son or daughter must be trained, like for instance the start of preschool, give yourself a good amount of leeway, or else have a backup childcare option available just in case. If you believe your response to any of the above sentences would be stress or anger toward your child, you will need to come to terms with that before you begin potty training. All of those scenarios (and even worse!) might actually happen, and all must be handled in a cool, calm, and collected manner. If there is anything about which you feel strongly, and with which your partner/spouse disagrees, now's the time to figure out a compromise.

From this point, you can start to formulate your stress-free potty-training plan. Your strategy shouldn't be too rigidly defined, because much will depend on how your particular child takes to the tactics outlined in this book. You'll want to make an educated choice about the ways in which you want to start, have a preferred timeline, and discuss your plan with all the parties who'll be involved (grandparents, babysitters, daycare, perhaps older siblings), but always keep in mind that your child is in control of this process. We know you are ready to do this, but before you begin to implement your plan, you'll have to determine if your son or daughter is ready.

Mom's Notes

Dad's Notes

2

Determining Readiness

P otty training is a process without an exactly defined beginning. It starts long before your child is actually attempting to go on the potty and includes a variety of motor skills, understanding, and interest. Your child's readiness forms the basis for those potty-related skills that will be learned during the training process: knowing and telling you when he has to go, stopping what he's doing to go, wiping, flushing and washing hands.

Determining the appropriate time in your child's life to begin teaching potty-training skills is key to your success, but it is also a very subjective determination. For many parents, there is a good amount of time between your toddler's initial interest in potty-related activities and actually training him/her how to use the potty. Throughout, it's important for you to set the stage appropriately.

The parent wanting to pursue potty training in a careful, thoughtful manner that takes into account their child's individual needs should consider the emotional, cognitive, and physical signs of readiness, as well as any outside influences such as daycare guidelines, school deadlines, the imminent arrival of a new sibling, a move, or planned vacation. There is no limit on what can affect this process, and thinking ahead may save you from a setback or interruption later.

- **Physical Readiness**—the physical milestones that should be reached before toilet training begins.
- **Cognitive Readiness**—an understanding of the concepts involved in going to the bathroom.
- **Emotional Readiness**—the most complicated to gauge, this involves how much desire your child has to potty train, and how much confidence they have in themselves.

This chapter delves into each of these types of readiness. We will also share scientific research on the acquisition of skills needed during toilet training and the average age of children when they master those skills. But first, let's discuss the time frame of the potty-training process.

Planning a Training Time Frame

There is no way to measure how long potty training will take. Some children learn faster than others, and parent reports range from weeks, months, or even more than a year. Obviously, you can't put your life on hold indefinitely, so once your child is receptive to the idea and participating fully, you should plan to have a good chunk of time, two to three weeks at least, to dedicate to the most intensive part of the training. That means two to three weeks of routine; nothing out of the ordinary. No vacations, no long trips in the car, no dinners out at restaurants, no birthday parties, no nothin'! Now, this doesn't mean you have to lock yourselves in the bathroom (although some parents have been known to do that!), just that you don't stray too far from your normal day-to-day schedule and familiar places—home and/or daycare should pretty much be it. Soon, you'll be able to ease them into going on potties other than the usual ones, but during this period, children may see each different toilet as a new challenge. You want to solidify their feelings of success on their own potty first, and then build up from there.

This two- to three-week period is not going to be the entire amount of time that goes into the training process. Setting the stage beforehand and continuity of lessons afterward can stretch the total out quite a while. But these weeks are a chance to powerfully establish the basics, and to assist as much as possible in the physical mechanics, of going on the potty. If you allow your child to tell you when he is ready, and then you are able to give him all the attention he needs during these intensive first few weeks, he'll be off to a great start. From then on out, you'll be constantly reinforcing what he's learned and adding more of the advanced skills to the mix.

But, let us not underestimate the importance of setting a good stage for the main show. The lead-up time to when your child jumps on board is what can take weeks or even months. This depends quite a bit on your child's age and personality type. It also depends on your ability to let your child take the lead.

Above everything else, please keep in mind that no person can force another to eat, sleep, or go to the bathroom. Strong-arming your child during any part of toilet training will not work; that will only cause stress and set you up for a series of power struggles over every session of sitting on the potty. All this can actually morph into more wrangling down the line with other parenting issues. This is not a situation you want to be in. From the mere fact that you're reading this book, we know you want to go about potty training in a thoughtful, caring, stress-free manner that will empower your child toward greater independence.

Parents are facilitators to the process of potty training—you don't control the process. In the end, your child will be toilet trained according to his or her schedule of readiness, not your agenda or timeline. However, using the strategies we give, you are giving your kids the opportunity to move the process more efficiently along than might otherwise happen if they are left to their own devices.

Toilet training isn't a subject that has been submitted to intense scientific study, but what little is out there suggests the normal age range for readiness is older than previously thought. One study published by a group of pediatricians from Wisconsin found the age to be 22–30 months for both boys and girls.[1] Regardless of the stories that you may hear of children who were potty trained at 24 months, 18 months, or even earlier, it is perfectly normal for a 3-year-old to not yet be out of diapers. Don't succumb to the pressure to start before your child is ready, as this will only set up a challenging, stressful situation for you and your child. What no study can tell you is when the right time will be for your individual child to start learning to go on the potty. That is a little up to you, but mostly up to your child.

What science can give you is knowledge about the steps other children follow when being potty trained. The study mentioned above found a sequenced order in which toileting skills are acquired. There are just

---

[1] Schum, Kolb, McAuliffe, Simms, Underhill, and Lewis, "Sequential Acquisition of Toilet-Training Skills: A Descriptive Study of Gender and Age Differences in Normal Children," *Pediatrics,* March 2002.

slight variations in gender, and for each skill a range of ages is given. Please keep in mind these ages are averages, and do not say anything about what is "normal" development. Your child may very well learn according to these age ranges, but you shouldn't worry if they achieve these skills a little earlier or later than the children in this study.

What we particularly like about this study's findings, to which we'll refer from now on as the Skills Acquisition Chart, seen on page 26, are the age-range guidance for parents, the breakdown of each individual skill that goes into the overall potty-training process, and the order in which they are usually learned. As parents, we often have to keep our eye on the big picture, but it's the small details that matter most to a child. Thinking of this as a series of small steps will make the entire experience easier for everyone.

And it's possible your child is already well on his or her way, having already learned some of the twenty-eight skills defined in the study. For instance, the first is staying bowel movement–free overnight. Some babies are already at this stage; their natural body rhythms regulate this. Your toddler may also have some of the other early skills by now, such as knowing potty words and telling when he goes. So, you may well start with one of the first couple of skills listed in this chart already checked off—that's gotta feel good!

There are a number of physical, cognitive, and emotional prerequisites that should be considered before you begin potty training. Each of these is important for different reasons, and some weigh more heavily with different personality types.

Physical Readiness

We already mentioned the natural regulation of your child's bowel movements, or poops, and the earliest toileting skill as being poop-free during the night. This is significant because it means the muscles are starting to develop enough to have an effect on elimination. At this stage of life, your baby or toddler cannot consciously control these muscles yet, but that skill is coming soon.

TABLE 1. Ages of Attaining Toilet–Training Skills by Gender

Toilet-Training Skill	Median Ages (in months)	
	Girls	Boys
Stays BM free overnight	22.1	24.7
Understands potty words	22.8	24.5
Has potty chair/seat available	23.2	25.2
Shows interest in using the potty	24.1	26.2
Tells during or after having a BM	24.6	27.0
Has regular BMs	24.9	26.2
Stays dry for over 2 hours	26.0	28.9
Indicates the physical need to go to the bathroom	26.3	29.3
Sits on potty when placed for 5 minutes	26.7	31.2
Flushes the toilet by self	26.8	27.0
Tells during or after peeing	28.4	32.6
Knows how to urinate in the potty	28.8	30.9
Washes hands by self	29.4	31.7
Pulls training pants or underwear up by self	29.5	33.5
Urinates in potty with help	29.7	31.7
Pulls training pants or underwear down by self	29.7	32.8
Wears training pants or underwear	30.9	33.8
Tells before having a BM	31.0	33.6
Uses regular toilet without a potty seat	31.4	34.0
Stays BM free during the day	31.5	34.7
Tells before having to urinate	31.9	34.7
Wipes urine effectively by herself	32.2	NA
Urinates while standing by himself	NA	38.0
Stays dry during the day	32.5	35.0
Enters bathroom and urinates by self	33.0	37.1
Wakes up dry overnight	34.1	35.8
Enters bathroom and has BM by self	34.4	39.5
Wipes poop effectively by self	48.5	45.1

NA, not applicable.
Sequential Acquisition of Toilet-Training Skills: A Descriptive Study of Gender and Age Differences in Normal Children, by Schum, Kob, McAuliffe, Simms, Underhill, & Lewis, Pediatrics, March 2002, used with permission.

Other physical milestones that should be reached before toilet training begins involve the fine and gross motor skills needed to get the job done. Your child must be able to remove her clothes. The last thing you want is for an accident to happen simply because she's unable to get her pants off quickly enough. This can be very defeating for a child. She must also be able to climb up onto the toilet. This can be daunting, but if she is already climbing on other things (jungle gym, the furniture), you can rest assured she'll get the hang of the toilet fairly soon. A step stool will help her reach both the toilet and the sink for handwashing afterward. Even if you choose to start her on a potty chair at first, she should still be physically able to get onto the big toilet.

Other potty-training books and many medical experts include the physical marker of waking up dry from a nap as necessary before starting the process. We don't believe this is a real-world indicator. Most children relax so deeply during REM cycles that they would be physically unable to control their bladder. The goal of the initial skills of potty training is being able to stay dry during the day, and this really has no bearing on sleeping time. Being able to hold it overnight or during a nap comes later, sometimes much later. At this point, naps, or at least the ones that are good for something, should not require dryness. However, if your child is waking up dry from his nap, you've got a bonafide sign he is ready for training. If not, those same books and experts usually qualify this prerequisite with, "naptime dryness or the ability to stay dry for two consecutive hours during the day." What all of this means is that your pediatrician wants to know your child is starting to flex his bladder muscles. How can you tell? Do a quick check of his diaper every fifteen minutes or so during the day. If you can't open it up that often, just listen to hear if the diaper crinkles when you push on it, which will mean it's dry. If your child is in daycare, ask the caregivers to try to do this as well. Usually, daycares will write down diaper contents at each change, but this won't tell you a whole lot about how long he's able to go in between regular changes. You might also consider buying less-absorbent diapers at this point, which will allow you to feel more readily if she is wet or dry, and more importantly, allow her to feel the wetness.

This brings us nicely to the next physical sign of readiness, which is that your child can feel when he is wet or dirty. Does he get uncomfortable when he's sitting in a poopy diaper or does he play happily along, oblivious to the stinky mess beneath him? Does she feel the added weight of the pee in her diaper and ask for a change? Perhaps he goes off into a corner or special hiding place when he poops? Or maybe she comes to a complete stop in whatever she's doing and gets a funny look on her face when she's going? Pay attention to your child's signs of elimination and label these out loud for him or her when you see them.

Potty Talk

Mom: You are scrunching up your face so hard, you must be going poop right now!

Dad: Wow, you just shivered and it's not even cold. I'll bet you were going pee-pee just then!

Also, during diaper changes, point out whether there is pee or poop in the diaper. Many kids will become curious and want to look at their diaper contents, which is fine. This can also be a terrific opportunity to start emptying the poop from the diaper into the toilet and allowing them to flush it away. This will get them involved in the process, albeit in a very small part, but it's one way of setting the stage for the training that is to come.

While you're watching for these physical signs, try to gauge whether your kid has a regular elimination schedule. For instance, some children poop 15 minutes after a meal, like clockwork. The act of eating and swallowing triggers the movement of everything through the intestines to make room for the new meal to be digested. Most children, whether they are controlling their bladder or not, go pee when they wake up from overnight or a nap. Whether it's the sensation of peeing that wakes them up or they wake up to pee, we'll never know, but it's a natural schedule to be on. Other children just get on some sort of circadian rhythm in which they have a bowel movement at one particular time every single day. Checking diapers a lot more often will give you a good idea of when they regularly pee and poop. It also may be that your child doesn't seem to have a regular schedule, and, although it doesn't help your plans along any, that's okay too.

Cognitive Readiness

Having an understanding of the concepts involved in going to the bathroom is another form of readiness. When children grasp the basic idea of what pee and poop are, where they come from, and where they should go, children will then be able to comprehend the more complex notions of all this pertaining to their own bodies. And the more they understand, the more comfortable they will be taking control of the process.

Your son or daughter should also be able to talk, and ideally will already know the words for the parts of their bodies, as well as for peepee and poop. Developing a vocabulary is essential for effective and efficient communication about toileting. It doesn't really matter what words your family chooses to use, but the anatomically correct names of body parts will best serve the kids in the long run; if they use the correct terms for their body from the beginning, they'll be more comfortable taking responsibility for their own health in the future. Do make sure everyone in the family uses the same words, to avoid confusion. Your child should be able to communicate his diapering or toileting needs to you, but also understand and follow your directions.

Allowing your child to observe your acts of elimination in the bathroom is one of the most important ways to set the stage properly and encourage her interest in being just like mommy and daddy. She should at least know that grown-ups don't use diapers. If you aren't currently modeling good potty behavior, there's no time to start like today. We'll go through the reasons this is so important.

A child who has the awareness to tell you when she or he is wet or dirty and needs a diaper change is a child who, more than likely, is ready to start potty training. This kid is demonstrating her or his capacity to make the connection between the physical and the cognitive, and is then able to turn it into language to communicate needs.

Sometimes, children who have physical and cognitive readiness will express an interest in potty training on their own. This often takes parents by surprise, coming earlier than they expected it. While there's no specific time table, this seems to happen around the age of two in many cases.

This is exciting for parents and children alike, and there is often some success when they first start out. But when a child does not have the appropriate emotional readiness to truly potty train and sustain it, that success is short lived. Excitement quickly becomes frustration.

Parents whose child exhibits early success with physical and cognitive readiness—the ability to control his muscles and know what he is doing—need to remember that without emotional readiness the process will not be quick, easy, or completely successful.

Emotional Readiness

Emotions often run high during change-in-life transitions such as potty training, both for the parents and the child. A whole new world will be opening up, and each party intuitively understands this is a big deal. Emotional readiness signs are the most complicated to read in a child who cannot yet express complex feelings.

Before you commence with toilet training, your child should be secure in the love she/he gets from both parents and realize that love is not tied to succeeding at this new goal. Potty training is a process of skill acquisition that is unlikely to go perfectly. Your sons or daughters should be confident in their ability to master a talent they once found difficult. By that we mean they should have had to try and fail at something else before becoming proficient—and we're sure they've had oodles of opportunities. For example: sipping from a cup, scooping with a spoon, stacking a set of blocks, learning to shoot a basketball through a hoop, pedaling a tricycle, or pulling on pants or socks. She/he should feel safe being unsuccessful for a while and understand that a big skill like going on the potty will take practice to get right.

Learning any new skill is difficult; at first your child will probably fail (i.e., spill the juice down his shirt, not be able to get any cereal on the spoon, inadvertently topple the stack of blocks). A typical response can be emotional, but if you feel your child overreacts to making a mistake or not being able to do something right, then he may have a fear of failing. To a degree, that kind of an overreaction can instead be indicative of a Strong-Willed or Internalizing temperament, so be sure to read those chapters carefully. However, if this carries over into a reluctance to try anything new, that may be a sign your child is not yet emotionally ready to attempt something like potty training, in which there can be a great deal of failure before there is success.

If you think your child does have a fear of failing, the best thing you can do is make sure she sees, feels, and hears your unconditional, positive regard. Find something about each so-called "failure" and praise her for continuing to try. You should be particularly careful that you don't show strong emotional reactions to everyday failures when your child is in hearing range. And when the inevitable happens—the spill, the tower crashes, the button won't get through that tiny hole, etc.—your reaction should be calm, reassuring, and matter of fact. Persistence toward a goal, despite temporary frustrating setbacks, is what you want to cultivate in your child.

A much more subjective emotional sign of readiness is a child's desire to learn how to pee and poop like grown-ups do. If your little one is asking to use the potty or wear underpants, you're ahead of the game and may have an easy time of it. If this isn't happening yet, don't stress. We talk about ways to kick their interest into high gear throughout this book. At this point, we're assuming you haven't started potty training, and so a kid who's receptive to the idea may not be entirely sure what it means. Once you start the actual training, they may not be as keen on trying it. You still may need to ease them into it, and we'll give you tips on that as well.

If you've already made some overtures to your child about trying to go on the potty and were fiercely rebuffed, you should take that as a sign that they are not yet ready to start this process. You can still set the stage for readiness, and we'll outline some subtle ways you may try to nudge him or her in the direction of the bathroom.

We know just being parents in today's world means a bit of constant stress, but you really want to optimize your chances and not start potty training when there is a good possibility that it won't go well.

Stressful times often make us less-effective parents. It is important to plan potty training when things are relatively stable. So avoid starting the training when you've just had another baby, when the family has recently moved (or is about to move), or when things are otherwise in great flux. If you are thinking that your family life is always stressed out, then it is important that you address that as a problem rather than trying to squeeze one more difficult task into your already busy family life.

•••

The potty-training process involves more than just teaching the physical actions taken in the bathroom. It encompasses emotional and cognitive readiness. After reading this chapter, you should have an understanding of what readiness looks like in a child and be able to gauge where your child fits in this spectrum. If your child is ready in all aspects, then by all means jump right into full potty-training mode. However, if your child still needs time in any of the three areas outlined—physical, emotional and cognitive—you can still *begin* the process.

In the next chapter, we'll take you through what we call our Universal Strategies. These are the most basic parenting tools and techniques; the building blocks of a positive parent-child relationship in which knowledge is shared and skills are learned. While we've tailored all of these strategies specifically toward the potty training process, they are the foundation of all parenting. With this first major milestone of independent behavior—learning to choose to go to the bathroom on the toilet—your child will learn his or her first lessons on what it means to be a big kid and a member of society. Regardless of whether your child is ready now or still has a way to go, the following chapters will help you plan your next move.

3

Applying Universal Strategies

So, you're confident your son or daughter has an appropriate level of comprehension about the process and is both physically and emotionally ready to start potty training. Congratulations! You're about to embark on a new chapter in your child's life.

This requires careful planning about how you will approach the subject for the first time with your child. Potty training is exciting for you because you know what to expect—a more independent child, lower grocery bills, and the removal of a messy duty from your roster of parental responsibilities (at least down the line, as most children require help in wiping themselves until they are into their fourth year). But again, we ask you to consider this from your child's point of view. He's about to unlearn skills he thought he had down pat—peeing and pooping into a diaper. He's being asked to climb up to and sit on a large, slippery, cold thing that makes scary noises as it takes his pee-pee and poop away to a mysterious place. You may be laughing as you read this description, but some children really stress about the toilet in this way!

Throughout this book, we'll examine five common personality types in children, in conjunction with what makes them tick, what makes them mad, and what will most effectively encourage them. You'll need to apply what we give you to your individual daughter or son. There are no perfect methods that will work for every child, and there are no guarantees as to which of our suggestions will spur your child to the bathroom and toilet.

In this chapter, we'll outline some of the most frequently used Universal Strategies that work with most children. Then, in the following chapters, we'll break them down even further and discuss subtle ways you can tailor them to your child's temperament.

Universal Strategies are the best actions you can take toward potty training. These involve increasing the likelihood that your child will decide that going on the potty is a worthwhile endeavor. Express to them the natural incentives for using the potty—becoming a big kid, being successful at achieving a goal, exerting control over his or her body, and getting out of diapers. Setting the stage properly involves role modeling, a relaxed atmosphere about potty training, some props, an accurate reading of your child's natural temperament, and, then, some flexibility on your part.

After the stage is set, you'll move on to the first steps of potty training. This almost always means teaching your daughter or son the physical act of peeing in the potty. At this point, that's the only goal. Then, you move onto helping him or her learn how to flex those muscles and hold the pee in until she/he can get to the potty. After that, you and your child will work on staying dry during the day and, eventually, wearing big girl or big boy underwear. Naps and overnights shouldn't count at first. Accidents will happen during sleep cycles when your child is most relaxed, even with the easiest children to train. (Some children sleep more deeply than others; some will get the hang of nighttime dryness soon after they can hold their urine during the day, and others will not be able to control those muscles during sleep for a long time.) After your kid is successfully in underwear during the day and not regularly having accidents, you can then start getting her comfortable going poop in the potty. And, then, the last skill most children learn is how to wipe the poop effectively.

The stress-free techniques for toilet training in this book have been proven to work for other parents, ourselves included. You can combine them as you see fit, skip any that you don't like, or just use bits and pieces of them.

So, let's start off with some of those Universal Strategies!

Keep Perspective

Potty training is among the first developmental challenges that seem to resonate for everyone. There's the first day of school, first date, first kiss, first day of college—all of these first milestones. But, for many, the first of the first is potty training. This is also why parents get stressed about it: it sometimes feels like one of the first public "good parent or not-so-good parent" moments.

But that feeling, the one where you feel that success or failure in your parenting skills hinges on whether your child is still wearing a diaper, is a fabrication. Kids who potty train a little later achieve just as much success in life as those who potty train early. There's no correlation between the age at which a child potty trains and achievement as an older child or adult. And so, you should understand that whether or not your child is wearing a diaper, is *not* a commentary on your parenting skills. It may seem as if it is, and indeed some other parents, usually those whose want to feel superior about the fact that their children trained earlier, feed into that, but don't buy into it.

Resist comparisons to other children's progress; each child potty trains at his or her own pace and progresses differently. Barring serious medical or developmental difficulties, there is no scenario in which your child does not learn how to go to the bathroom. Whether he makes it there with the understanding and encouragement of his parents is something that must be safeguarded by you and depends on your attitude about the process.

A parent's consistent focus must be on the long-term goal of raising an independent, kind, strong, and successful person, who is also able to complete personal toileting tasks. Think of potty training as just one short-term goal along the way to that long-term goal. Each step in the potty-training process, no matter how small, must be appreciated and celebrated as part of the journey. At the same time, each setback or challenge must be dealt with in a manner that is mindful of your toddler's emerging personality and encouraging of the potty-training process as a whole. Feelings of despair over the progress your child is making toward that goal must not be allowed to take root.

While parents must focus on the end goal, they should not allow that focus to crowd out anything else their child is interested in, doing well at, or showing improvement in, because that will not help move the potty-training process forward. Even the youngest of children will sense if a parent makes the achievement of potty training too important, and that can actually derail the process. Keeping perspective and keeping potty training stress free means acknowledging that training is a learning process.

Communicate Clearly

Whenever a person is trying to learn something new, clear communication of the vocabulary, directions, and expectations is essential. It helps avoid misunderstandings and ensures that you know what you're supposed to do. Think about the last time you tried to learn something without clear directions, and you'll understand why communication is so important to your child—not just for the potty-training process, but for anything else they'll need to learn.

Teach your child the correct words for body parts and functions, and then use those words consistently so he or she understand them. Start this when they're very small, particularly during diaper changes. They'll start to pick it up. Certainly use these words well before you start potty training in earnest, because just having the right words will help them get closer to cognitive readiness, if they aren't already there. If your child is a little older, don't despair; it's never too late to teach them the right words and for you to use them throughout this process. Using the anatomically correct words helps children grow comfortable with these words and starts them on a path to being able to take charge of their bodies from a young age. Comfort with their bodies is important later on when they are talking with doctors and can even make them less vulnerable to abuse.

Sometimes, in this book, we will recount the types of conversations many parents have had with their children during potty training. At other times, we'll suggest dialogue that you might want to try with your child. Please use these dialogues if they are helpful, but also make them your own. Put your own personal twist on the conversations, tweak them for your child's age and level of development, and insert your own terms of endearment or family traditions. These are guidelines and ideas that we hope are helpful to you, but we certainly don't expect you to use them as exact scripts.

Here are some tips for communicating clearly with your child, based on age:

➤ 2-year olds—Keep words and sentences very short and repeat them often. Use the five senses to attach meaning to those words and phrases. Books are a great way to highlight the words they are learning.

- 2½-year olds—The verbal range at this age is very wide, but if your child is using words consistently, you can now start to lengthen your sentences a bit and use some adjectives to go along with those words they know.
- 3-year olds—Continue with the same words, but build up concepts by using more descriptive words. This is the age where "Why?" becomes the child's reply to everything. Try to answer every "why" without frustration.
- 4-year olds—Real conversations are now possible, as they have many more words and understand concepts reasonably well.

Be a Potty Role Model

Being a parent means being a role model 24/7. Everything you do will cement itself in your child's mind as the way things should be done. Children are keen observers, often noticing the unconscious habits of the adults in their lives. Way beyond overtly teaching them how they should use the toilet, the way you approach the task yourself will set the tone for your children.

To do this, you will need to sometimes leave the bathroom door open while you do your business. If your child is like most, you probably won't have to invite him in to observe; he'll probably already have trailed you in there. Because she/he is going to be asked to copy what you are doing, it's important to try to role model your bathroom activities along same-gender lines as much as possible, at least at first. It doesn't need to be exclusive, but primarily dads should show their sons and moms should show their daughters the right way to go potty. Of course, in a one-parent household it may not be possible, but initial role modeling will be most effective with the same-gender parent whenever available. Also, if one parent objects to allowing their opposite-gender child to see their private parts, those feelings should be respected by all.

You don't have to have an open door, all-access policy in your bathroom, however. Potty role modeling will foster teachable moments in the bathroom, and this is an extremely effective way to activate your child's interest in the matter.

Depending on your family's dynamic, once the initial impression has been made with the same–gender parent, you can keep role modeling restricted, or you can get everyone involved. Watching the way older siblings, playmates, and even pets go to the bathroom will also stimulate your toddler's curiosity. The benefit of involving siblings and friends is obvious; if your child sees kids she looks up to doing it, she may want to imitate their behavior. It might be easy for the toddler to emulate older siblings in the same household, but you'll still want to supervise and make sure the older children are actually modeling the correct habits. If they aren't, or if they don't like the idea of letting their little brother or sister watch, then they don't need to be involved. Older brothers and sisters should never be required to be a part of the toilet-teaching process. Obviously, though, good behavior toward their younger sibling, can and should be required. Potty training within a multichild household needs to be balanced with whatever appropriate establishment of privacy rules and boundaries work for your family.

The Dirty Diaper

Thirteen-year-old Quentin is a terrific big brother to two-and-a-half-year-old Tariq—pitching endless baseballs to hit, pretending to be a favorite superhero, and even singing kiddie songs like, *The Wheels on the Bus,* with gusto. Quentin is a great babysitter; he even changes diapers! When the time came for Tariq to be potty trained, however, Quentin decided this wasn't something he wanted to be involved in. Their mother, Shari, intuitively understood her oldest son's reluctance, even if he didn't express it. The age of thirteen is rife with plenty of adolescent angst about bodily changes, and Quentin wasn't comfortable being observed so closely by his baby brother. Quentin continued all the playtime activities, but as much as possible sidestepped the potty training. The boys' dad, James, was Tariq's primary role model, and naturally so.

If the people living in your household extend past the parents and siblings of the child being potty trained, use your best judgment regarding who should participate and who should not. At least educate them on what you're planning to do to ensure they won't sabotage your carefully designed efforts. (We're thinking specifically of grandparents who may try to force or shame the child into sitting on the toilet—that's the way it was often done in their day, but it's not something you have to accept or want to encourage.)

Make sure everyone involved understands what you want them to do. And, in the end, it is fine if modeling is kept solely between the child and the same-gender parent, as it meets the goal of showing him or her how it's done.

– – – – – – Training Tip – – – – – – – – – – – – – – – –

Because it won't be long after potty training when your child will start being excluded from the bathroom, offer an explanation of privacy at some point during this process.

– – – – – – Training Tip – – – – – – – – – – – – – – – –

This is the time when most pediatricians recommend discussing personal safety issues—that is, certain body parts are private and only mommy or daddy (or a doctor with mommy or daddy) should ever touch you in those places. If needed, ask your family pediatrician to help you start this conversation.

We recommend that parents talk out loud about what they are doing when role modeling in the bathroom so the child can listen without having to participate at first. Try to anticipate your child's concerns and address them before questions are asked. Be matter of fact about what is happening, answer questions in a straightforward manner, and keep your tone light and friendly. As awkward and gross as it may seem, consider showing your child your pee and poop. Let him flush it down for you, if he wants.

For some kids, the big toilet brings out some nightmares. We've heard of kids thinking there is a monster in there, kids who are afraid of the noise or even the bright lights in the bathroom, and kids who are afraid they'll get sucked down into the drain. Dispel any far-reaching fears or misconceptions your child may have about the toilet. Frank, informational dialogue should continue throughout potty training, and can become the foundation of effective parent/child communication for highly personal subject matters.

Potty Talk

Mom: Mommy needs to go pee-pee, so I'm going to sit on the potty and listen. . . . Can you hear the pee-pee going into the potty? You make pee-pee in your diaper, but someday you'll be a big girl, and you'll be able to pee-pee on the potty, too!

Dad: Wow, I really have to go pee-pee. I'd better run to the bathroom. [Upon arriving:] Whew! I made it. Now I just have to pull down my pants, point, and . . . here comes the pee-pee!

If this causes your child to want to try, you can sit him on the toilet, naked or in a diaper, to let him see what it's like. Because a child's natural curiosity can lead him to try this on his own, and because children of this age can easily fall into a toilet and drown, you should always make sure they are properly supervised in the bathroom and that the toilet is kept off limits when you're not there.

Training Tip

If you have a baby-proof lock on the toilet, when the time comes for the actual potty training to begin, you'll obviously need to remove it. But never leave your child alone in the bathroom until you are comfortable she can manage getting on and off the toilet safely.

Potty role modeling doesn't have to be all about humans, either. As strange as it may sound, your family's pet can also set a good example for your child, or at least give him some additional knowledge about and opportunity to observe the acts. You can make the analogy to teaching the dog or cat where to go. Puppies and kittens are born going wherever, just like babies. But as they get a little older, we teach them where to go: in a litter box, on some newspapers, or outdoors. If you don't have pets, make a few potty comments during a trip to the zoo or point out bird poop on the sidewalk. The lesson is, every living thing has to eliminate waste, and your child is no different. Going to the bathroom is natural, and although it might be a little scary at first, it's something every person and animal learns how to do.

As you progress in discussing bathroom habits with your toddler or preschooler, talk about more than just the act of going.

➤ Describe the signals your body sends to tell you it's almost time to go.
➤ Explain the way you use your bladder or rectal muscles to hold in the pee-pee or poop until you can get to the potty.
➤ Talk about how you attempt to go before you leave the house for a length of time so you don't have to interrupt a fun activity.
➤ Tell them about what it was like for you to learn how to go in the toilet. Now, we know you probably don't really remember, but it's perfectly acceptable to make up some stories about common things that happen or specific aspects of toileting you think will give your child particular difficulty. Here are some suggestions you might want to try.

Potty Talk

Mom: I remember when I was a little girl and I had an accident once in the supermarket. I was trying to hold in the pee-

Dad: pee until we could get to the bathroom, but I couldn't. It came right out, all over my underwear and my dress. That made me really sad, but my mommy—Grandma—told me it was okay, that happens to everyone sometimes, and she helped me get all cleaned up.

Dad: Ready to go to the football game? Uh-oh, it's going to be a long time before we can go to the potty, so I think I'm going to try to go pee-pee right now. That way we won't have to leave the game early. I remember once when I was a little boy and my dad had taken me to a football game, we couldn't find the bathroom at the stadium! Oh my gosh, it took so long that my tummy muscles started to ache from holding the pee-pee in, but we finally found it. It felt really good to go potty that day.

Mom: When I was your age and I was learning to pee-pee in the potty, I was really nervous about the toilet in my grandmother's house. You know why? Because it was green!! Back then, they made toilets that were green, blue, and even orange! The green ones were pretty scary to me. You're lucky because when you learn to go you'll be able to use a plain white toilet. (Of course, if you or a family member happens to still have a green toilet, you'll want to amend this one!)

Role modeling these sorts of things for your child makes him feel more comfortable and relaxed because he knows that these were skills you had to learn as well. Understanding this, he may open up to you about his concerns and fears down the road. In addition, all these conversations will likely stick in his mind for a while, and saying them now gives you the opportunity to bring them up at apropos moments later on when your child may need a reminder of the lessons you learned as a child.

Give Good Directions

For any task they learn, children need simple, clear, understandable directions. Because we adults don't really think about going to the bathroom and eliminating waste into a toilet—it's a process that is ingrained in our behavior and virtually unconscious—it can be difficult to give the kind of directions our children need to successfully learn, especially at first. This is why role modeling good potty behavior is so important. You'll be doing all the steps for your child to replicate, even if you don't think to express them in words.

Good, clear directions will reduce miscommunication and frustration, avoid some potentially messy situations, and also build his or her sense of his or her own competence, which is important for developing self-esteem.

Here are some tips on how to give effective potty training directions:

- ➤ Ensure you have your child's attention.
- ➤ Use age-appropriate communication techniques (see Universal Strategy of Clear Communication, page 37).
- ➤ Break down the process step by step. Because some of these steps may be taken unconsciously by adults after doing them for so many years, it can be helpful to physically show your child what to do, as well as explain verbally.
- ➤ Offer a positive outcome, using *if/then* and *after/then* statements, which tie an outcome to a behavior. For example: "*After* you try to go potty, *then* we will be able to go out to the park."
- ➤ Keep your instructions short and simple and have your child repeat them or paraphrase back to you to ensure they are understood.
- ➤ Always finish with praise.

Some kids just simply "get" everything to do with potty training from day one. They take to it like fish to water—peeing on the potty, pooping on the potty, even controlling their bladders overnight. Success, voila!

Alas, many other kids don't. For them, the idea of going on the potty is new and different and even overwhelming for some. They can't wrap their mind around the various expectations and so refuse to have anything to do with it. This may happen because they were not ready to start potty training, they just didn't realize everything that is involved in learning this skill, or they are just slow to adopt new ways of doing things.

If you think your child isn't ready, you should not push. Instead, give her some time. You can shift into low gear and focus on the Universal Strategies of Clear Communications and Role Modeling for the time being. These may feel very subtle to you, but can be very stimulating and motivating to a child. In fact, we don't ever advocate doing nothing, so you should always be using these strategies to move the potty-training process forward, even if your child isn't ready for the more physical learning.

If he is overwhelmed, break the process down into separate teaching elements. Let him learn to pee on the toilet first, then maybe something a little easier like washing hands (rubbing soap around for one chorus of the Happy Birthday song is a fun way to ensure cleanliness). After these two goals are reached, and your child has a sense of accomplishment, you can progress into teaching him how to poop on the potty.

For teaching most children, it is best to treat peeing and pooping as separate, although related, activites. Different muscles are used, different sensory and even emotional factors come into play, and your child may have very different reactions to the training.

Once she/he is firmly established at peeing and pooping into the potty, you can begin to think about going for nighttime dryness. Breaking it down into sections like this will help you in your teaching techniques. Let her see how great it feels to be successful in the basics first, which is essential to her self-confidence. Then you can build on that success toward the more complex elements of toileting.

You may think it'll take longer for your child to master potty training if you teach it in phases, but consider the alternative—power struggles, meltdowns, unhappy children, frustrated parents, and failure. The best way to train is to build on a series of successes rather than by eliminating one failure at a time. Every step forward is a step in the right direction, no matter how big or small a step it is.

Act Like a Coach

A parent is a child's first coach, in everything. Coaches cheer team members on, but also teach the skills that still need to be learned. Potty training is a great time to put this concept into motion. Just make sure your coaching mentality is age appropriate: we're talking little league, not NFL.

The coaching strategy consists of a discussion with your child just before he or she starts to learn a new skill. You need to recap the wins she's already had (skills already learned) and then be very specific in terms of letting her know what you want her to do.

For example, if your child tends to hold his pee until the last moment and then has an accident, you need to be proactive and say exactly that:

> Mom: *"You're doing such a great job knowing when you have to go, but we don't always make it to the bathroom on time. So, today, we're going to try to start heading to the bathroom early. Let's work on paying attention to what your body is telling you. I'll check in with you every 15 minutes and ask you to concentrate on your body for a minute. If you feel like you might need to go, you can try right then. I'll bet we have a great day without too many accidents! Are you ready to start?"*

You are soliciting your child's agreement that he will work on the skill that you have very specifically named. In an encouraging way, you've pointed out where his weakness is and given him the tools to overcome that weakness. Bringing it to his conscious awareness before the accident occurs makes it more likely he'll be able to learn how to pay attention to his body's cues on his own. Those regular prompts every 15 minutes (you can set your own intervals) will be helpful to direct his focus.

Keep in mind that a coaching job is for the long haul, not just one season. With the higher end toileting skills, the most coaching needs to occur. And just like coaching a sports team, your child isn't necessarily going to get every concept the first time. Every team will have setbacks.

A good coaching technique for validating your child's feelings when an accident does happen is to personalize your empathy.

Dad: "It's okay, when Daddy was a little boy, I used to have accidents, too."

Mom: "Clean up time. Do you want to sing the clean-up song with me?

Letting your child know that you have had the same emotion she is having is a powerful lesson. In using validating statements, you're identifying with her emotions, and then coaching her on how to learn from setbacks or failures.

Determine Your Child's Schedule

Many babies' natural body rhythms start to revolve involuntarily around a regular schedule. Savvy parents can capitalize on this when they are ready to start training, but you have to observe the patterns well before training begins. Keeping a chart can be helpful, but for most parents, it's simply a matter of paying a little closer attention to the time they change diapers each day.

It's much easier to check the pooping patterns, as that is easily gauged by smell and sight. Some children will poop right after meals. Others poop once a day at generally the same time. A urination schedule is harder to determine, but if you start checking diapers and changing them more often, you'll get a much better feel for how often your child pees. Your daycare provider probably records diaper changes, so you can ask for assistance in determining patterns.

Figuring out if your child is on a schedule means you can choose those times of the day when your child is more likely to go as the time to use a training technique. It'll just stack the odds more in your favor if you have an event to use as a teaching tool.

Although some kids are on a schedule, many others are not, so don't despair if yours falls into the latter category. Although a set schedule is helpful, it is not a prerequisite to potty training. You will just have to be a bit more patient in waiting for results. Once you have an understanding of his schedule, or lack thereof, you can use it to your advantage with these next two related Universal Strategies:

Hop on the Pot

One commonsense approach to toilet teaching is to make a routine of sitting your child on the potty first thing in the morning, after every meal, and before bedtime. Even if he doesn't produce anything worthy of a flush, this technique will get him used to the idea of trying at regular intervals during the day. Using this as an early technique with your young toddler, even before actual potty training starts, can stave off some of the hang-ups you may encounter in an older child who sits on the toilet for the first time. Setting this up as the de facto routine can be a preemptive strike against any fussing or power struggles. If your child has been sitting on the toilet several times a day for as long as he or she can remember, it simply becomes another thing that is done in your house, like brushing teeth and taking a bath. Routine makes the process predictable and normal. Similar to a schedule in many daycare centers, even the Strong-Willed Child doesn't necessarily resist because it's what everyone does every single day. As with everything, don't force your child to sit; however, if you start this habit before it occurs to him to resist, you'll be ahead of the game.

Some parents take this method to a higher level with an intensive potty-training schedule of sitting on the toilet (or potty chair) every twenty or thirty minutes. They set the alarm on their cellphones, watches, or even the kitchen stoves and, every time it rings, they bring their child into the bathroom for a minute of trying to go potty. Because of the rigorous pace, this doesn't teach your child a whole lot more beyond following your directions. This can be a strategy to use, but take care to consider whether your child's temperament will allow for it. If she resists, a more relaxed form of scheduling will be better used in conjunction with other techniques.

As with all of these toilet-training strategies, parents need to consider their own personality type in addition to their child's. For example, Goal-Directed and Strong-Willed Parents are more likely to want to undertake the demanding "all-at-once" approach, but this might not work very well if your child is Sensory-Oriented or an Internalizer. Strong-Willed Children, in particular, would be antagonized by your attempts at such strict control. Others, such as Goal–Directed Children, may revel in the concentrated sessions.

If your child does show some reluctance, never force her to sit on the potty. Major resistance should almost always be treated as a time to back off. There are other ways to entice her onto the toilet, but you may just have to wait until she's ready.

Hold Practice Sessions

Hand in hand with the Universal Strategy of coaching is the idea of holding practice sessions. Now, you may think that potty training is just one great, big practice session, but what we're suggesting is a much more deliberate strategy with the sole purpose of helping your child become familiar with the process. It's a great way to get him started.

Begin by giving him your full attention, with no other children around, and practice at a time when you have no scheduled activities or deadlines. Explain this is just practice and that it's not a real drill right now, but you want to show him what will happen when he starts to learn how to go on the potty.

Take him through the entire process from feeling the urge to go, rushing into the bathroom, pulling down pants, sitting, pushing, wiping, pulling up pants, flushing, and washing hands. Have him take the actions but don't expect any results at this point. This is only practice. Repeat your run through once or twice more (depending on whether you still have your child's attention), and try to point out some different things each time.

You can spend time practicing each day or a few times over a week for as long as you feel your child is getting information from your potty practice sessions. In at least one practice session, mimic what happens during an accident. This can preemptively take the sting out of a real accident, since the practice session shows your child it's a possibility and it won't be as scary as if it happens to them out of the blue.

The beauty of practice sessions is that they build familiarity with the process and, since there are no expectations for performance, it's stress-free (although you may get lucky and actually have success in one, which can be very empowering for your child). Practice sessions give your child a positive, successful experience that you can then remind her of before the next "real" situation. These sessions give you a calm setting in which to show your child what to expect during this situation. They also give you an opportunity to see what hurdles you might be able to mitigate, as, for example wearing looser clothing so that pulling pants down and back up becomes a great deal easier for your child.

Additionally, practice sessions can be a tool to use in the middle of potty training. For example, if she's stuck on a particular skill, you can stop regular training to conduct a practice session on that skill alone (or group it with one or two more from a similar point on the Skill Acquisition Chart on page 26) which can give your child the boost she needs to get it down. This break can also serve as a way to de-stress if getting stuck on that skill has her upset or worried. When she's not stressed, she can learn easier.

Another benefit is that practice sessions allow you to rehearse keeping your priorities in perspective when facing an accident. You will learn just as much from these practice sessions as your child in terms of managing your own responses. Practice sessions can require a significant time commitment, but they are one of the most helpful strategies for parents and children.

All of the strategies outlined thus far—Be a Potty Role Model, Keep Focus on the Goal, Give Good Directions, Act Like a Coach, and Hold Practice Sessions—all will be strengthened by an infusion of the next strategy of using positive reinforcement.

Offer Positive Reinforcement or Rewards

Positive reinforcement refers to anything that increases the likelihood of a behavior. In the language of psychology, the sequence of antecedent-behavior-consequence is a key to figuring out why people do what they do. The consequence part is where positive reinforcement can happen. The parent suggests the child use the potty (antecedent), he uses the potty (target behavior), and he's praised contingent upon his demonstration of the target behavior (consequence). If a child uses the potty and is praised, the consequence (praise) increases the likelihood that he will use the potty again. Positive statements, praise, and hugs should be provided every time your child tries, or is successful on, the potty. It will empower your child to own this process, and it's the best way to spur him ever forward to becoming completely potty trained.

The ramifications for positively reinforcing good behavior in this manner extend well beyond potty training. You will be molding your child into the kind of person who is intrinsically motivated, ambitious, and persistent. He will attribute success to his own effort. Gratification comes from a job well done, and failure results in more effort as he possesses the confidence to succeed independently. Positive reinforcement ingrains this kind of attitude into your child's very nature, and it will serve him well into adulthood. The second book in our Stress–Free Parent series, *Stress-Free Discipline,* discusses positive reinforcement a great deal. Using it correctly during potty training sets you up for more successes in shaping your child's behavior during other stressful times, such as temper tantrums, meals, and bedtime, as well as later on with homework and attitude.

Because rewards like candies or toys can create extrinsic, or derived, motivation in the short term, parents may tend to use them for everything. It's an easy trap to fall into: "If you sit nicely in the shopping cart, I'll get you a treat when we check out," or "If you play nicely with your cousin, I'll buy you a new toy on the way home." We're not immune to using this kind of lure occasionally. However, constant use of external rewards can suppress the development of independence and sense of achievement. Their behavior becomes all about the "thing" they get rather than just being the right thing to do.

For potty training, a consequence like praise is different from tangible rewards, such as the ever-popular M&Ms® or stickers. Both are reinforcing to a very young child, and the little candies may be more potent in the short term, but the behavior is associated with the M&M only. Positive statements, praise, and hugs are much more potent in the long run and will be more likely to stimulate the intrinsic motivation that we all want our kids to have because they represent something much more valuable than a tiny piece of chocolate—our respect and admiration. Any child's desire for this grows—more so than her desire for another M&M.

Praise is not only healthier, but there is an inexhaustible, free supply of it. We always have some with us. As parents, it also gives us the chance to specifically target what we really want to reinforce—our kid's effort, willingness, and interest. Based on our feedback, our children will begin to value the same traits we are reinforcing—persistence, tolerance, overcoming frustration, patience, bravery, commitment to a goal, and so on. Reinforcing all of that can be done quickly and efficiently in a statement of admiration or even a quick burst of applause. The very best time to start working on the development of an internal achievement mindset in a child is early childhood!

However, there are times when an external reward is appropriate, if used in the correct manner. By tying the reinforcer (reward) to the specific potty skill learned, you also teach your child about good consequences stemming from his actions. It all comes down to how you set up the child to earn a reward.

Here is an example of what we mean: let's say a child expresses interest in the hottest kiddie movie coming soon to a nearby theater. One option would be to use the movie as a simple reward—giving something of value to the child for doing something you ask. However, in this case, if you tie the outing to your child's efforts at potty training, you can drive home the importance of the skills your child is learning: *after* you learn how to go on the potty, *then* we will go to the movie. You'll recall such after/then statements are one of the ways to Give Good Directions. Here's one way you could explain it:

Dad: Wow, that does look like a cool movie, and I can't wait to take you as soon as you're going pee-pee on the potty all the time. We can't really go to a movie this exciting if you're still wearing diapers, because we'd have to change you, and we'd miss half the movie!

So, in both cases, the parent takes the child to the movie based on successful potty training, but instead of using it as a tangible reward for the child doing what the parent wants, the reward is presented as a natural consequence of the child's accomplishment. In this way, she/he retains ownership and learns a longer term lesson. There is no judgment involved in this dialogue. Instead, after the child has stated an interest, the parent simply links it to potty training and points out the natural contingency. Of course, parents are always free to stoke the fires of interest by exposing their kids to interesting and potentially rewarding things. After all, without some level of exposure, what does a three-year-old know about going to the movies? You can change this reward to an ice cream party or a trip to the zoo, whatever you think will resonate with your child. This is best done at random intervals—and it can improve the potency of the daily praise, which is understandably less flashy of a reward.

An outing like a feature-length movie could be tried after a couple of successful weeks of staying dry in underwear during the day. This shouldn't be an early reward after a day or two of going potty, as you might be setting him up to have an accident in public, which will only set back the process.

Dad: Back when you were wearing diapers we couldn't go to movies like this. Now that you are using the potty, it makes it a lot easier to go to big kid places. I'm really glad you are using the potty, because I love doing special things like this with you.

The above conversation would work well in the restroom, while trying to go potty just before the movie starts. Cause and effect, behavior and consequence—it's all about positive reinforcement.

Beyond making the decision to use praise rather than rewards to encourage your child, you need to consider that there are multiple types of praise, so using the correct kind of praise to reinforce your particular child's desired behavior is also of critical importance. Everyone has individual preferences that dictate what kinds of things will be reinforcing to them. This is particularly true of children. Some like lots of excited praise, whereas others like quiet statements of pride and are in fact turned off by overly animated statements.

Sensory-Oriented Kids might not like a lot of physical contact, whereas an Internalizer and an Impulsive Kid might find greater reinforcement in hugs and cuddling.

Both the Goal-Directed Child and the Strong-Willed Child will be driven by the successful accomplishment of the goal, but you have to be careful that the Strong-Willed Kid doesn't think you're encroaching on his or her success.

There's no best universal way to praise a child, and thus reinforce behavior. You just have to read yours, taking her temperament into account, and then go with whatever seems to most effectively encourage the behavior you are trying to teach. Make your praise specific to her behavior at that moment, and try very hard not to raise your expectations the instant one small goal is met. You'll also need to adjust the kind of feedback you give to be appropriate to your child's actions. For example, after she's been peeing in the potty productively for a while, an excited response will lose its potency. That's not to say you stop the praise, but you must tailor it to fit her skill level.

Nakedtime

Nakedtime is one of our favorite methods for beginning potty training. Basically, the idea is that you allow your child to simply be naked, but in fairly close proximity to a bathroom or potty chair, for periods of time during which (we hope) they will need to go. To your child, it's tons of fun, and perhaps something she/he hasn't been able to do before. To you, it's a fantastic teaching tool with the following benefits:

➤ Nakedtime is nonthreatening and passive; when you start, you don't even have to mention that it has anything to do with going potty.

➤ It's a natural introduction to toileting.

➤ With no clothes on, kids have, for the first time, a clear view of the physical mechanics of urination and defecation.

➤ You can provide immediate explanations of what's happening, demystifying the process and breaking it down into simple, specific behaviors your child can learn one at a time.

➤ You, too, will have a clear view of your child's body language, and can more closely read the signs of impending elimination.

➤ Without the barrier of a diaper between your child and the toilet, results can come quickly.

Nakedtime is a very useful and simple tool for parents to use to potty train. It is nonthreatening to the child and involves no cajoling or power struggles. Because you are simply removing the barriers between your child and his or her physical elimination process, nakedtime brings out the instinctive and intuitive reactions we want our children to learn. Nakedtime for toddlers or preschoolers demonstrates the cause and effect of the biology of the body—drinking and eating leads to digestion which triggers elimination in the form of pee and poop—and physically trains them to recognize the signs of having to go and eventually hold it until they can get to the potty.

Because they don't have any clothes on, their attention will be focused on the mechanics of elimination and they will actually see and feel the results immediately. Getting the diaper out of the picture will help them make the connection between the urge to go, the actual act, and, at first, the cleanup. Training your child naked, as opposed to simply dressing her in clothes with underwear, also means the lesson doesn't get entangled in clothes that are hard to pull down; you both can focus on the first skill of getting the pee-pee into the potty. Once your son or daughter is successful in that, you can move on to teaching the next skills. Wet or dirty clothes are powerful motivators for your child to regularly go on the toilet, but they have to know how to do that first.

If you're not a stay-at-home parent, planning nakedtime sessions during weekends or an at-home vacation should give you a very good start on potty training. Remember, the nakedtime technique first teaches the primary step of getting the pee into the toilet. Learning to pee in the potty is a very important start. If you do it for much of the day, every day you have available, your child will have peed or pooped enough to get the main point. From there, your childcare provider can help you along the process by layering his or her techniques over yours.

Nakedtime can be messy, but if you orchestrate it carefully, you'll be able to avoid any permanent damage to your home. Because toilet training is something that should take place close to home, at least initially, consider allowing some nakedtime around the house, or if you have the space, in the backyard.

Now, we know some people may be nervous, for various reasons, about having a naked child running around all over the place. Perhaps you're worried what your neighbors will say or about soiling an expensive carpet, or you feel you'll be teaching them impolite behaviors. Regardless of the reason, if this strategy makes you at all uncomfortable, then you can amend it to be simply an extension of bath time or you can skip it all together.

Backyard nakedtime during the warm weather months is a wonderful potty-training opportunity that makes for easy cleanup, thus reducing stress for parents. Additionally, it's fun. Get a kiddie pool and let your child fill it with the hose. Buy a party-size bottle of bubble fluid and have at it. Popsicles can drip all they want—there are no clothes to stain.

Safety during nakedtime in the backyard is paramount. We recommend shoes, to reduce the chances for injury. Choose sandals, water shoes, or something easily cleanable (even old sneakers you're about to toss out) because they will probably get dirty during an accident. Are your kids prone to sunburn? Sunscreen is a must regardless, but if your child is very fair, you may not want to expose him to the sun during the hottest part of the day. An outgrown t-shirt may be just the trick to shade his torso, while still leaving the lower half easily accessible. (A regular or long t-shirt may get in the way and become wet.) Do you have a mulched area around a swing set where splinters could poke a sensitive area? If so, you'll probably want to restrict nakedtime to another part of the yard. If you determine that your child can safely use a swing set during nakedtime, you'll need to be extra vigilant about falls. Sliding would probably best be avoided, as would riding a bike.

If you hold nakedtime sessions indoors, obviously, you're going to want to consider whether you have surfaces or carpeting you don't want soiled under any circumstances. It'll be best to stay out of these areas at least until you get a feel for how receptive your child will be to this potty-training technique and how quickly she'll pick it up. If your bathroom and kitchen are close together, you could probably figure out inventive ways to corral her during the nakedtime sessions. Be sure to take another look at how secure the baby-proofing is in these areas, because having to call Poison Control will put a serious dent in the potty training. Another option for indoor nakedtime is to simply extend bath time in the bathroom, perhaps by as much as an hour, so that it's more likely she'll need to go while you're in there.

If your child has a regular schedule of eliminating, we suggest co-ordinating nakedtime sessions for when he or she is more likely to go. If your child doesn't have a regular schedule, simply begin at a convenient time. Plan to start with peeing first, although of course you can never be sure this will be the first to happen. You can try to increase the odds by giving an extra cup of water before or during nakedtime.

When introducing the idea of nakedtime, parents should not present it as having anything to do with potty training. One of the best reasons for using this technique is that it is very passive and natural, so you should protect that atmosphere.

Potty Talk

Mom: Hey sweetie, what if I let you do something silly? Wanna play this morning without wearing any clothes?

Dad: You don't want to get dressed in the clothes I picked out for you? How about if you just wear your birthday suit then?

Mom: Oh no, we don't have any clean clothes for you today! Well, I guess you're going to have to be naked for a little while until we can get this laundry washed!

Without any pressure, your child, even one who's been reluctant to try to go on the potty, will be able to subtly begin training. To them, running around naked is just a new way to play, but as soon as the first accident happens, they slip naturally into potty training.

The first accident can't really be considered an accident, because they haven't yet learned the correct behavior. Because you aren't letting them know this fun nude game is about potty training, the first time they pee or poop during nakedtime will serve as the introduction to the *idea* of going on the potty. When your son or daughter goes, you should point it out in a matter-of-fact tone and explain that happens with everyone. At this point, your child will be more likely to really listen to and absorb the overarching biological lesson you give him/her. Typically, kids don't like having pee or poop all over themselves, and so you can naturally and casually show them where the potty is and how they can use that the next time so it won't be so messy. This first "accident" is all about observation and the dawning of knowledge.

At first, when your son or daughter pees, you'll probably have to point it out—she or he may not even notice it is happening until they feel it start to trickle down their legs. Most likely, they will not be able to stop mid-stream. Recognize this and talk them through it.

Potty Talk

Mom: Oh, look, honey, you're going pee-pee.

Child: (upset) Mommy!!

Mom: That's okay. We can clean you up real quick. You know, if that happens again we can run superfast to the bathroom, and you can go in there just like I do. [Or, if you're already in the bathroom: When this happens, you can just sit on the potty like Mommy does. Do you want to try that now?]

Many children will be distressed by the pee running down their legs at first, and you should react with the same calm, relaxed demeanor you have when talking about anything potty related. If your child hasn't yet tried to sit on the toilet, now is a good time to broach the subject, but do not unexpectedly put them on there while they are already dealing with the stress of their first accident. Offer the option of trying it right now; there is a chance your child tensed up enough to stop their stream and perhaps has a little more pee they can put into the potty—and hurrah, you have a fantastic experience upon which to kick off your potty training in earnest. If, however, your child recoils from your suggestion to sit on the potty, respond in the same composed manner, "That's okay, maybe you'll want to next time."

Determine before you start nakedtime how you'll go about clean-ups, both of the liquid and solid variety, so you aren't caught off guard. Have supplies close by, so you can tend to both your child's emotional disappointment at an accident as well as your own need to do a fast cleanup job. Do not blame your daughter or son if their bodily fluids do any serious damage to a floor covering or anything else. After all, you're the one who took the diaper off knowing full well she or he doesn't know how to control those muscles yet. Cleaning should be matter of fact; don't make a big deal about it.

Repeat all of the above with each nakedtime session, and build up from every success. Take something positive from each session, and praise her for this effort. If, for instance, she started to realize she had to pee, but didn't quite make it to the potty on time, you should tell her what a great job she's doing recognizing the signs her body gives her when she has to go. If your son peed in the toilet two out of four tries, make a big deal to your spouse or partner that he did it twice! (Some kids even want to save their pee or poops for mommy or daddy to see when they get home, which is fantastic because it means they've made this a goal.) You can acknowledge the two failures or ignore them based on which response will best suit your child's personality, and then move forward. If your child has no successes on a particular day, give him a thumbs up anyway and let him know you are proud of him for trying. Keep your expecta-tions to yourself and remain unruffled about setbacks. Praise your child's efforts in an authentic, meaningful way to positively reinforce their good behavior. Continue to identify the signs and feelings of needing to pee so that your child will be able to start to recognize them.

Outside of the nakedtime sessions, you can continue to keep your child in diapers until you feel like he or she is making some headway. Nakedtime is for studying their own body language, and for realizing when their bladder is full, how to control it (and the colon too, although pooping can be left for later lessons if it doesn't naturally become a part of nakedtime), and hold the pee until they get to the bathroom. Once

STRESS-FREE POTTY TRAINING

you introduce underwear, the focus of training will become more about holding it for longer periods of time and trying to go even when they may not feel like it.

As great as nakedtime is as a teaching tool, there will come a time when it won't be as useful. If you feel like no headway is being made, you can discontinue the sessions or put them on hold for a while to try some other strategies.

There may also come a time when your child (often the boys, purely for physiological reasons, but this does also happen with girls) starts to spray or play with their waste. Although this can be aggravating and just plain gross, it may indicate some success in your teaching method. If your son or daughter is engaging in purposeful peeing or pooping, that should be evidence that the child understands the mechanics of the process and has some element of control. Parents don't need to get into a big fuss about the mess, but we would suggest restricting or eliminating naked-time at this point—it will have served its purpose for potty training and will instead deteriorate into peeing or pooping just for fun, or to press parents' buttons.

Although nakedtime is a good method to use with almost any child, there are specific ways to best approach and manage it with each personality type. We'll more thoroughly explore the differences within the chapters dedicated to each personality type, but here are a few things to keep in mind:

➤ If **Goal-Oriented Children** take to this, it has the potential for an intensive training session in which they quickly progress through nearly all the steps.

➤ **Sensory-Oriented Children** could become extremely upset with the mess, so we suggest warning them about that in advance, which could head off this problem.

➤ **Internalizers** may not be comfortable if nakedtime is done where people can see them, so you should make sure the area is a private backyard or indoors.

➤ **Impulsive Children** will probably love nakedtime and take to it very quickly, but do not jump to the conclusion they are fully trained.

Consistent and constant follow-up is needed to reinforce this newly learned behavior.

➤ **Strong-Willed Children**, in particular, need to remain in the driver's seat when it comes to potty training, so if they tell you they want to put their diaper back on, allow them to do so; you can try nakedtime again another day.

Props

A terrific way to set the stage for your child to become interested in potty training is the use of props. Apps, websites, books, videos, and dolls are all appropriate and useful tools. Reading storybooks about using the potty—specifically about other children using the potty—is a great way to introduce your child to the idea.

Apps and Websites

Members of this generation are called digital natives. Babies come out of the womb seemingly able to access technology better than most adults. As a result, it may be very natural for your child to expect and use virtual assistance in potty training. There are apps for every mobile platform, and websites to boot. Some are designed to be entertaining and informative to children, while others are schedule assistants or chart trackers for parents. Any and all can be useful, depending on your needs.

Augmenting your potty training routine with the help of an app or website may work to your and your child's advantage. For example, parents just starting out in the potty-training phase may want to chart their child's elimination schedule to get a feel for whether there are predictable times when she'll pee or poop, thereby allowing parents to concentrate potty activities during those times. Others will allow you to set an alarm to indicate that it's time to try, cueing you and your child to head to the bathroom. If your child, especially if he's an Impulsive Child, has a hard time sitting on the potty for enough time to produce anything, a game on a handheld device could give him the extra time necessary for a success.

Given that we're talking about young children holding on to a costly electronic item while hovering over a big bowl of water, it would make a great deal of sense to take precautions against a dropped device. Ideally, a parent should be sitting right next to their child on the potty and holding the device so it doesn't fall. At the very least, you should be able to grab your child or the device if the balancing becomes precarious. Bringing a lapdesk into the bathroom could also be a good idea, so there's something upon which the device would land before hitting the toilet water. Investing in a waterproof case might be another choice, especially if the device is new or expensive.

It's worth noting here that we aren't advocating starting your children off using mobile devices and playing video games this early in their lives. There is scientific evidence that excessive play may negatively affect aspects of cognitive and social development. However, we are also parents ourselves, and thus we are realists. Most children are allowed to use their parent's device at one point or another, often when they are being expected to sit still. Obviously, those times when your child is on the potty qualify, and so use of a device may be a good short-term tactic. You're in need of a distraction device for a few minutes, and it's no different than handing them something else to look at.

To be clear, we're not advocating your young child be given free rein on your mobile device. It's possible that kids will become so transfixed on the device that they won't notice when they have peed or pooped. A parent should make sure their child can still focus on the mechanics of going on the potty. Additionally, you don't want your child to have a permanent association between your device and going potty. Impulsive Kids, in particular, are notorious for later gravitating to video game/television over practically everything else because they are easy stimulation. Bottom line is that a game app your child likes can be useful, but just like anything else, don't overdo it.

There are more apps and websites than we could list here, and they are changing constantly. Find some that work for you, but do try to remember that potty training encompasses a great deal more than any app or website gimmicks or games alone. These devices can only enhance, not replace, the time and energy that a parent needs to invest in the process with their child.

The Dirty Diaper

Since we're talking about apps and devices in this section, we would be remiss if we didn't include a warning about posting potty training photos of your child on your social media accounts. Please refrain from doing this, for a number of reasons. First, you are creating the beginnings of a permanent digital record for your child. Pictures of them on the toilet, in various stages of undress, or just after either a success or an accident, are not things they will want included when a future employer searches their name online. Second, there are some twisted individuals online who get aroused by young children in various stages of undress, some of whom search out potty training pictures in particular. No parent wants a photo of their child to be used in that manner. Third, when you are posting a photo of your child potty training, you are not concentrating on your child at that moment. During this process, your child needs your attention to be on him or her 100 percent of the time.

Books and Videos

The pictures in the book, probably even more than the words, will provide a great deal of fodder for him to consider.

You can't really go wrong in choosing one of these books. A good, inexpensive way to see whether a book resonates with your child is to check it out from the library. Some librarians may even have a list of the most popular ones for your convenience. Many of these books are differentiated by gender, and if this is your first child, choose the correct one. If this is your second (or beyond) child, and you already have a book but it is now being used by a child of the opposite gender, don't sweat it. The idea is simply to spark your child's interest, and the pictures don't have to match their bodies exactly.

When you read the books, stick to the story and be careful not to change it to be all about how your child will someday do this, too. That might be too much pressure. However, you can ask your child what he thinks about the story. Point to the illustrations and ask him to tell you what's happening, even before you read the book for the first time. This will likely give you some good insights into his thought process at this point. If he jumps up after reading the book and heads to the bathroom to try it for himself, that's a clear sign he's ready for you to start his training. If he asks questions about what happened to the child in the story, you should answer in a relaxed manner, and can casually suggest he give it a try if he wants. If he does, great; if not, don't stress. Just try again after a few days. If your child simply moves onto another activity after the book, give him some time and see if he comes back to you later. Again, if he does, great; if not, don't worry. You can try setting the stage in another way or see if he wants to read the book again after a couple of days.

Many storybooks come with accompanying videos. If he expresses interest in the book, it is a good idea to give the video a try. Of course, books have the added benefit of promoting literacy, but videos can reinforce the same idea.

Potty Chairs and Toilet Rings

Potty chairs and toilet rings are props that can complete the scene setting. Miniature versions of the toilet, potty chairs can be comforting to a child intimidated by the real thing. They look very cute and nonthreatening, they are low so kids' feet can touch the ground, and they don't make any scary flushing noises. Having a child-size, portable pot for your toddler or preschooler to use anywhere, anytime, can help her ease into the course of action. At first, it'll be a fun new "toy" on which your child will want to play potty. You can get one and have it around as early as you like, as long as there are no expectations for her to use it. The potty chair can then be used in conjunction with any of our other suggested strategies and can even be carted around with you on outings or long trips in the car after your child is trained but when you may need a quick pit stop.

A toilet ring is what you place on top of a regular toilet to make the opening a little smaller, and thus more stable, for your child. The fun colors and designs, along with the extra padding, may help your child feel a bit more comfortable. They can be portable as well (and there are specific fold-up kinds to fit inconspicuously into a diaper bag).

Dolls

Dolls can be terrific tools to show both boys and girls the mechanics of toileting. There are special potty-training dolls on the market, and those are fine, but you can really use any doll to the same effect. They can help you show your child more about the what, where, and how of potty training, but be sure to explain that dolls don't always have the same body parts that real people have. Many children will "play potty" with their dolls, mimicking your lessons. You could even join in and act out a potty scenario. Ask your child to help explain to the doll about going on the potty and see what she says. Children will often repeat what you say to them, sometimes even word for word and tone for tone. Listening to how they talk privately to their dolls can give you great insight into your teaching effectiveness. It's interesting to hear what they take in and what they think is important to "teach" their dolls. You might discover your child's potty-training fears by hearing her console her dolls' fears. Later on, when it's your child who's scared or worried or has an accident, you can recall what she said to the dolls to make them feel better.

If your child resists any of these props, don't push them. The aim here is subtlety, If they don't take to the books, videos, potty chairs, or dolls, then set them aside for a little while. You may be surprised a couple weeks later to have your child choose that book to read before bedtime or pick up the doll and sit her on the potty. Allowing your child's interest to develop naturally is what will work best for a quick and painless potty-training process.

Introducing Underwear

Introduce the idea of wearing underwear once you're comfortable your child is having some success in flexing his bladder muscles. Present it as an incentive to continue his efforts, and tie it to the concept of "trying" to go potty even when he doesn't feel like he has to go.

Potty Talk

Dad: Look, buddy, I got some big-boy underwear for you to put on since you're getting so good at going pee-pee on the potty. But there are some rules about wearing underwear that all big boys and girls have to know. When you're wearing underwear, you are going to need to sit on the potty sometimes even when you don't feel like you have to go pee-pee. Sometimes it will come out and sometimes it won't be ready, and either way it's okay. So, if you think you can follow my directions and try when I tell you it's time to try, then we can put this new underwear on you! Do you think you can do that?

Child: Yes!*

Dad: Okay, then, let's put 'em on. Wow, you look so grown up without a diaper on!

*Alternate scenario,

Child: No, I don't want to!

Dad: Okay, bud, no problem. I'll put the underwear right in your drawer until you're ready, alright?

Underwear is a big step in a child's life. It feels different to walk, run, sit, play, and even fall down—in short, everything changes. At first, you might want to let your daughter or son try on their big-kid underwear for a few minutes. If they like them, they can keep them on for a while, but this is a perfect opportunity for you to tie this benefit to trying to go potty. As long as they try to go when you tell them to, they can keep wearing their new undies—and it doesn't matter whether they actually produce anything in the potty at this point, it's the attempt that is the key.

Take the progression from diapers to underwear as fast or slow as your child dictates. This is a turning point in the toilet-training process, from which there is no going back, and so your child needs to accept the responsibility on his or her own terms. At this moment, your child is probably not yet ready to tackle nighttime dryness, and so will wear a diaper to bed at night. Many children will go pee as they wake up, so it will behoove both of you to get that diaper off as quickly as possible in the morning in hopes of getting the day's first pee into the potty.

As soon as they can show you a measure of bladder control and the desire to wear big-kid underwear, there should be no going back to diapers during the day. Once that overnight diaper is off, another doesn't go on until bedtime. There is no need for discussion or negotiation on this point, assuming your child was ready. It should simply become your new routine. If you need to make the point more obvious, start buying a new brand or color of training diapers and explain that these are special and only for nighttime. You could also keep them in a special nighttime box that can only be opened at 8:00 p.m., or whenever bedtime occurs in your house. In the event that your child is getting the hang of bladder control very quickly, and you notice the diaper is dry each morning, you could choose to work toward nighttime dryness as well. Just make sure your expectations are not exceeding your child's capacity for change. In other words, don't push it. Nighttime dryness is an advanced toileting skill, usually not mastered until the end of the potty-training process.

We aren't big fans of the so-called "No More Diaper" parties in which parents throw a celebration for their child's rite of passage into wearing underwear because this puts the emphasis on the diaper—which is by now a thing of the past—instead of on the future. The better positive reinforcing tool would be something like an outing or event to which they would not have been able to go if they were still in diapers.

In addition, going without diapers cold turkey on a predetermined day, such as a birthday, is going to set you up for power struggles with your child, and you should avoid this at all costs. Therefore, we don't recommend this approach. Some parents have amended this method to become a countdown to "no more diapers" and have had some success, but this kind of external pressure on the child may be too much for their little shoulders to bear.

Handling Accidents

Accidents will happen with every child. They are inevitable and are actually an essential part of the potty-training process. Just like other skills kids eventually master—stacking blocks, throwing a ball, pulling on their clothes—they gain knowledge from trial and error; they learn from their mistakes.

That's not to say, of course, that parents should encourage accidents. Quite the contrary. If it doesn't happen very often, it is less tolerated by the child, and so she/he thereby has an increased incentive to avoid it in the future. Many types of children are liable to have an extremely adverse reaction to accidents, especially if they are repeated on a regular basis, and this does nothing to help potty training along. Sometimes, recurrent accidents will completely stall the drive to learn toileting skills, and you may find your child actually regressing.

A parent's reaction to their child's first failure will set the tone for the rest of this process, so think very carefully and plan how you'll respond. A relaxed, matter-of-fact manner will say a great deal before you say anything. You should be expecting the accident, whereas the child will not. So, try to keep your body language under control. Your voice should remain calm, you should not grab your child roughly (even to yank him off the new carpeting), and your eyes should meet your child's to convey a team spirit. What you are communicating is that you are in this together and you will stand by and assist your daughter or son with whatever they need.

Try to gauge you child's anxiety level; it may or may not be high. In fact, if this is the first accident, she may not even realize what's happening. Your first step might be simply to clue her in.

Mom: Oh, you're going pee-pee. That's okay, sweetie, it's just an accident. Don't worry, I'll get you all cleaned up.

If she isn't all that upset, just change her and continue on with whatever you were doing. Depending on the strategies you're using, you might want to mention that the next time this happens, she could try to stop the pee-pee from coming out and run to the bathroom.

But, if your child is scared or anxious about having an accident, you'll want to be sure to comfort him as best you can with a big hug and some calming words. Clean him up and change his clothes as quickly as you can if this is what seems to be bothering him the most. If you plan ahead for this occurrence, wipes or paper towels will be just an arm's reach away.

After the first time, parents can start to turn accidents into learning experiences. Talk to your kid about her bladder and rectal muscles and give her an idea of how to flex these muscles to hold the pee-pee or poop in. Have a secret signal she can give you so that you know she needs to go. Come up with a silly rhyme to sing as you rush, rush, rush into the bathroom. The act of running itself will help take her mind off her bursting bladder and can give you just enough time to get her to the bathroom. Because praise is what will reinforce behavior, try to find some positive feedback to give your child after an accident. It doesn't need to be very much.

Potty Talk

Dad: I liked that you ran so fast to try to get to the potty on time! Next time, I bet you'll make it in time.

Mom: Wow, you got your clothes off all by yourself—you didn't even get them wet. You came really close to getting the pee-pee in the potty this time.

Expressing your confidence in your child's ability to do better next time is a good way to positively reinforce the behavior. You don't want to pay too much attention to the accidents because some children crave attention, and if they see this is a way to get it, they will continue to have accidents. However, just because your child regularly pees their pants doesn't mean he or she is being willful. It may be a case of starting before he/she is really ready, difficulty controlling the muscles, a lack of interest, or a deficient understanding of the signals the body gives off. Stepping up the role modeling may help in all of these situations.

Depending on their child's reaction, parents might need to think about accidents from a different perspective. In other words, rather than looking at an accident as a potty-training issue, parents might think of it as a lesson in frustration tolerance and resilience.

Depending on the dynamic between some children and their parents, it might be best to basically ignore recurring accidents, cleaning them up without much comment. If you're apt to become upset, bite your tongue and say nothing instead of something that will increase your child's anxiety or discomfort. Perhaps you'll end up needing to discuss the situation with your spouse and ask that they take over the training for a little while.

Know When to Back Off

Sometimes your child will react as you expected, but other times fierce resistance will come out of the blue. Regardless of how it happens, the best course of action is always to back off and give your son or daughter some time.

It may be there are latent personality traits bubbling to the surface. It may be something about that particular lesson or experience that frightened him. Or there could be an outside influence at work—older children, television, a misunderstanding—that is scaring your child. It could also be an absolute indifference to the process! There are a million reasons why a kid might resist. Although parents should always put on their thinking caps and try to figure out the genesis of resistance, plenty of times the underlying reason is not evident. Kids this age may not be very good at really articulating what's at the root, even the ones who have pretty good verbal skills.

Resistance should not be interpreted as rebellion. Many parents, when they meet with opposition, are quick to jump into the power play and assume their child is being willful or difficult. In some cases, acting as if he is being willful may actually lead him into more strong-willed types of behavior. Reading your child's temperament and responding accordingly will help you tremendously in sorting through their reluctance.

However, regardless of whether you think you know the reasons for your child's reluctance, the best thing you can do is to back off, at least for a little while. Acknowledge his right, as an individual person, to stop the lesson for the moment. Pressing on will only entrench his reaction and set you back a couple hundred more diapers.

If something like this happens, check in with your child in ten minutes and then at half-hour intervals. You'll want to ease back into the aborted lesson or possibly even put it off for the remainder of the day. It's perfectly all right to gently ask what scared her. Give her as much time as she needs to get the words out or explain what happened. Don't interrupt with your ideas of what's bothering her. Let her explain, if she can.

Sometimes it's a serious problem, but other times it isn't. Don't jump to conclusions; you may be surprised by the cause of the episode. Plenty of parents will assume their kids were scared by the flushing sound, mad because they peed all over the place, or afraid a poop will hurt. More often than not, these ideas haven't even occurred to your potty-training novice and your guesses will simply give him ammunition for next time's excuse. Let your child explain. Only then will you truly be able to remedy the situation. For instance, it may just be a matter of turning the doll's head so it's not staring as he goes or getting out a new pair of underwear because the ones he had on "got a little bit wet."

It will also help to alleviate fears if you relate whatever she is nervous about to something that is more familiar to her. It may be that if you remind her that you used to have accidents the same way when you were a kid, she'll feel better about herself. You might also use a favorite game or movie to ease her fears. For example, the movie Frozen has the "Let It Go!" song, which can be comforting to a child worried about flushing her poop away. That song actually has a great many potty-training connotations, so use it as often as you can stand to hear it.

Advanced Skills

As your child masters the basic skills involved in potty training, you can continue to refer back to the Skills Acquisition Chart chart on page 26 to see what step to tackle next. Typically, the bulk of potty training involves your child's ability to control the bladder, recognize and respond appropriately to the signs of needing to go, and pee effectively into the toilet. Pooping into the potty is generally considered a more advanced skill, because it happens with less frequency. Wiping the poop is, according to the Skills Acquisition Chart, the last toileting skill attained by both boys and girls, around the time of their fourth birthday.

Pooping on the Potty

When proceeding to the next action, you can repeat the same kinds of stage-setting techniques amended to the specific skill you're teaching. Again, role modeling, discussion, and positive reinforcement are important. Be as precise and detailed as you can be with all of the above. Talk about the different kinds of signs your body provides to let you know there is an impending bowel movement. Explain again that poop is an accumulation of the waste products left over from digestion of food in whatever kind of language your child will understand or will spark their interest. Remind your child that every living being—people and animals— need to poop in addition to pee. Tell them that many people get on a fairly regular pooping schedule, once or twice a day. Watch to see whether your child's body is already regulating his or her output. Begin requesting your child to try to poop, either after each time she/he pees or at strategic times during the day when she/he is more likely to see results. Parents should again role model effective ways of sitting, pushing, wiping, and washing hands. In fact, this should have been ongoing since the first days of potty training, but at this point, you should step up your efforts as they relate to pooping. Repeat again and amend all these tactics to any next step you want your child to learn.

Wiping Poop

Wiping poop effectively is difficult for most children; the healthiest way to teach them to wipe is from front to back, but that can be tough to coordinate. For a while, you'll want to check to make sure they're getting it all. If some feces remain around their rectum, an uncomfortable rash or itchiness can ensue. If this happens, a little of the cream left over from your diaper days can soothe the area. Frequent bathing during the time your child is learning this skill will also help.

Some kids are incredibly disgusted by inadvertently getting poop on their hands and after that never even want to try to wipe themselves. Although it's important to educate your children about the germs contained within poop, you want to take care not to scare them too much. As with all the other issues involved in effective toilet training, if the parent takes on a matter-of-fact tone, they'll be able to convey the information and let the child determine his or her own emotional reaction.

Nighttime Dryness

Achieving nighttime dryness will be one of the last big hurdles to overcome. It's a daunting task for a parent: helping your child unconsciously control his or her bladder muscles during sleep. It is best if you can wait until this happens naturally and you start to notice dry diapers each morning. When this occurs, you can simply eliminate the diaper altogether and then deal with nighttime accidents in the same relaxed, matter-of-fact manner you did for daytime accidents.

To help the process along, you can reduce or eliminate drinks before bedtime. If your child is the type to continually ask for a glass of water while he is going to sleep, you can slowly start to limit his intake. As you do this, keep an eye on his morning diaper to see if this is the only trick needed to get the job done.

Some parents may want to plan to wake their child and sit them on the potty once or twice during the night. Just be careful, because waking a child at night can cause an already overtired parent to become more easily frustrated, and this will not help the greater effort. If you feel you must, prepare your child for this by explaining what you are going to do. Tell them during the day before you first start this practice. Remind them as they are going to bed so they will not be too surprised. However, by the time they're in the middle of their REM cycle, they won't remember your warnings, so you should wake them gently, assure them everything is all right, remind them of the plan, and then calmly steer them to the bathroom. If you can avoid waking them fully, you can teach them the art of unconsciously getting up to go. This may take quite a bit of repetition before they get the hang of this, however. Beware the child who will get the hang of waking halfway and heading to the bathroom, but not being awake enough to actually make it to the potty before they start to go. This is much more of a potential problem for boys just pointing and going, rather than girls who generally can recognize the feeling of sitting on the potty before they allow the stream of pee to start. Plenty of little boys have mistaken a plant, chair, or another item for the potty in their half-awakened state. Just like with daytime accidents, treat this with the same kind of sensitivity and positive reinforcement. Depending on your child and the situation, you may want to delay any real discussion of what happened until the next morning when your child can be fully awake and alert. However, if your daughter or son does fully awaken after an accident, go ahead and give them the comfort and praise they may need to relax and fall back to sleep again.

Mom: You are doing such a great job getting up in the middle of the night when you have to go potty. It's okay that you had an accident last night; this is something that's really hard to learn. You'll get the hang of it very soon!

To minimize the stress of a midnight accident for both you and your child, you can layer his or her bed with a sheet, then a waterproof mattress pad on top of that, and then another bed sheet. This way, when an accident occurs, you can simply remove the top bed sheet and mattress pad and quickly get your child back to sleep on the remaining bed sheet. If your child has multiple accidents through the night, investing in additional mattress pads to add to the layers can make for an easy solution. The bulkiness of the bed linens may bother a Sensory-Oriented Child, but most other kids won't be disturbed by it.

There is no need to attempt to teach a lesson to your child in the middle of the night; make clean ups as trouble free as possible. The next morning, you can talk to your child about ways to eliminate accidents, stressing the amount of liquid your child consumes in the evening. One suggested compromise for bedtime drinks is to place a tiny cup (even a plastic doll's cup or a shot glass leftover from your party days) next to the sink for your child to use at the end of the night. This can be a fun, novel way for your child to feel like they're getting a drink of water when they need it, but in reality it will enable you to limit the amount ingested. Oftentimes, a child's bedtime request for a drink of water is really a stall tactic instead of the need for actual hydration.

Most children are naturally able to regulate their bladder overnight by age five, but if you don't see that occurring, talk with your pediatrician because there are other tactics, like a wetness alarm, that they may recommend.

------- Training Tips by Gender -----------

BOYS

➤ Start off teaching boys to pee sitting down, which will allow you to focus on lessons of recognizing the signs they have to go, making it to the toilet on time, and the mechanics of physically going.

➤ Make sure they are tall enough to be able to pee standing up (i.e., when they stand at the toilet, their penis needs to be able to reach over the lip of the toilet enough for them to be able to point it down into the potty); otherwise, you'll have a regular spray of urine to clean up after each pee. If they can't reach, but want to learn to go like Daddy, keep a small step stool next to the toilet or use a potty chair for the time-being.

➤ Toss some Cheerios® into the toilet to teach them to aim properly.

➤ If using a small mattress pad to guard against leaks, place it a little higher on the bed for a boy.

GIRLS

➤ Spraying urine can be an issue for girls, as well, if they are seated far back on the potty and are propping their legs far apart to steady themselves. Teach them to keep their legs together straight out over the potty to the lip of the seat, if this is a problem.

➤ Dresses can make for easy access and will save time because your child won't have to stop to pull down her pants; however, they can trip her up as she climbs onto the toilet. Dresses can also drag into the toilet water or get in the way of the stream of urine, so teach your little girl to tuck it up into the neck of the dress to keep it out of the way.

➤ Girls are particularly susceptible to urinary tract infections at this age, so work very hard to teach your daughter to wipe poop cleanly, from front to back. Alternatively, you can teach her to wipe her pee-pee first and then get a separate piece of toilet paper to wipe the poop.

•••

Now, having learned about the Universal Strategies of potty training, you have the tools to begin to plan the best approach for your child. From role modeling to coaching and practice sessions, nakedtime to props, and, eventually, advanced skills to nighttime dryness, an exciting new chapter in your child's life is about to start.

Remember, there's no perfect method for potty training every child, so what works in your sister-in-law's family may not necessarily work in yours. Your son or daughter is unique, and his or her individual needs, preferences, and challenges must be dealt with in a manner that takes that uniqueness into consideration.

In the following chapters, we'll explore all of the personality types outlined in Chapter 1, and consider the steps of the potty training process in the context of that temperament. You'll learn many differences in approach to each temperament type, in addition to specific challenges or potential pitfalls of which to beware.

4

The Goal-Directed Child

P arents of Goal-Directed Children often describe them as having one-track minds. They are persistent and focus on getting the object or goal of their desire. If she wants to put the ball through the basketball hoop, she'll keep trying until she makes that shot. If she decides the train tracks need to be redesigned, she'll sit at the train table for an hour carefully building them. If you tell her she can go to the park if she cleans up all her toys, she'll focus in on that task and get it done lickety-split.

In this chapter, we will explore what makes a Goal-Directed Child tick and how parents can apply that knowledge to teaching the potty training process. From setting the stage appropriately to using our Universal Strategies, you'll have the steps you need to take to start your child going on the potty.

The Goal-Directed Temperament

Often logical, even at a young age, the Goal-Directed Child can comprehend the natural sequence of achieving something. He knows you have to do X before you can do Y: you won't learn how to sink a basket immediately; you have to practice how to throw the ball. He may grasp sequential concepts as well: if you add a riser track for the train to go up the hill, you have to match it with another at the top to let the train come back down. And, he certainly comprehends the quid pro quo of rewards—he'll not only put all his toys away to earn a trip to the park, he'll line up all the stuffed animals by height and sort the blocks by color, for extra credit.

All this bodes well for you, oh lucky parent of a Goal-Directed Child! Yours are usually the easiest to potty train, and can even potentially train in one day if you set up your plan that way.

Now, we say usually because a child of any temperament can be unpredictable at times, and also because some kids masquerade as Goal-

Directed Children but are actually ruled by different personality traits. We'll get more into that at the end of this chapter; for now let's talk about the inner workings of the mind of your Goal-Directed Son or Daughter.

These kids are curious about how, why, where, and when things happen. They can be directed fairly readily. They like to know and understand things, and they're willing to invest the time it takes to learn to do things correctly. Also, they may not get as frustrated as easily as other personality types.

These kids also tend to like to please their parents. In short, a Goal-Directed Child is hard-wired to enjoy accomplishment. Similar to a Strong-Willed Child, the Goal-Directed Child will focus in on something and persist in accomplishing it; however, the Goal-Directed Child takes pleasure in the accomplishment, whereas the Strong-Willed Child is happy for having exerted control over the situation.

After you determine they are ready, Goal-Directed Children are often the easiest type to toilet train. They'll likely take to the idea enthusiastically. They may even take the lead. Point them in the direction of the toilet and they will very often focus in on what they need to do to get the job done. Explain what they will feel when they have to go and they'll become attuned to their body's signals. Prompt them to try before you head out of the house and they'll willingly comply. Encourage them to sit on the potty a while longer waiting for the poop, and they'll make up a song for the occasion.

Sometimes the Goal-Directed Child will decline initial efforts to potty train; parents should read this as a sign that the child is simply not ready. If this happens, back off and wait a while. Although she/he may obey your commands to use the potty, if she/he isn't truly ready, you will be setting yourself up for later power struggles with your child. When your child does become ready, the process is generally fairly quick and painless.

Setting the Stage

As discussed in Chapter 2, a parent's role in potty training is only as a facilitator. Parents don't control this process, no matter how much force they may try to exert. A child's body is their own, even at this young age, and no one can compel him or her to eat, sleep, or go to the bathroom if she/he doesn't want to. Usually, however, Goal-Directed Children are quick to attempt to do their parent's bidding, and so toilet training these kids is often much more about teaching them the mechanics instead of trying to cajole their initial interest.

All of the typical scene-setting props will likely be of interest to your child—from books to dolls to videos to potty chairs. Offer them at will, but don't feel obligated to purchase them all. Role modeling behavior can often have the same effect, but it is nice to mix it up every once and a while. If you bring something home and it doesn't immediately strike a chord, set it aside or put it on the bookshelf and perhaps soon his interest will be stimulated. On the other hand, you may find is wholly unnecessary to set any stage; your child may skip right to Act One.

Rewards and Positive Reinforcement

Many parents find rewards to be particularly effective with Goal-Directed Toddlers or Preschoolers. We're sure you've heard of friends or family who swear by the M&M method—give the child one M&M for successfully peeing on the potty, two for pooping. Quite possibly, you've also heard of this kind of system getting totally out of hand as the kids learn to up the ante for a job well done.

Despite its popularity, we are not big advocates of the M&M method. The fact is that Goal-Directed Children enjoy accomplishment on its own merits, and adapt to rewards based on how their parents dole them out. The joy of success may well be reward enough for your child, and capitalizing on this should really be your initial approach.

The social rewards of praise are what drive most Goal-Directed Children. As the name we've given them suggests, they are directed by the goal they've set for themselves, so slapping hands for a high-five or a literal pat on the back are really all that's necessary to encourage these kids forward. The added bonus is that by using this kind of reward system, you can avoid the kinds of power struggles that erupt when savvy negotiators (future lawyers, we're sure!) decide their poop should be worth ten M&Ms and won't go until that is what is promised to them. The next day, the demands go up again.

We know you're excited about the prospect of getting your daughter or son out of diapers. We know how much money you'll save when you no longer buy diapers, and we know you're sick of the changing table. We've been there ourselves! But, and we say this with clear hindsight, rewarding your children for a natural, physical event with candy or a new toy will only serve to set in their mind the idea that they should get something for everything they do. Within a few years, they'll be tucking a pearly white under their pillow with the expectation of getting twenty dollars from the Tooth Fairy! (And yes, we know multiple families in which this has happened!)

The Dirty Diaper

Motorcycles have always captured the imagination of little Sebastian. When his parents, Michael and Evie, were trying to encourage him to go poop in the potty, they promised that Santa would bring him a motorcycle for Christmas once he accomplished this goal. Mind you, it was June when they made this offer. But Sebastian wouldn't have any of it. He'd been going pee-pee in the potty for a number of months and was wearing underwear every day successfully, but would ask for a diaper when he needed to poop. His parents were, understandably, getting a little tired of this situation, but when Sebastian refused this offer they figured nothing would get him to poop on the potty, so they decided to just back off for a while and wait until he became interested on his own. (Can you predict where this is going?) Two days before Christmas, Evie was doing some last minute shopping when she got a phone call. It was Michael who was thrilled to report that Sebastian had gone poop on the potty all by himself! Their happiness was soon dampened when they realized that Sebastian's action stemmed from his memory of their promise and his belief that Santa would now be leaving a motorcycle under the tree. Evie went dashing

through the snow to three different toy stores before she found
one with ride-on motorcycles in stock.

As Michael and Evie found out, you need to be careful what you
promise. But whatever kind of positive reinforcement you choose, define
it from the start, for yourself and your child. Make sure you're on the
same page with your spouse and/or childcare providers, and communicate your plan to any adults who regularly care for your child, such as
grandparents or a neighbor. You don't have to be tied to the tactics your
daycare uses—there is a much different dynamic between training one
child and training a class of fifteen separate personalities. Although you
should be aware of their system and be prepared to interweave it with
your own, most children of potty-training ages can differentiate between
the way things are done at school and the way they're done at home, as
long as neither of you work against the other's efforts.

Praise should be liberal, but always sincere. Don't go overboard
because you're excited, but do make your child feel great about learning,
share her enthusiasm about becoming a big kid, and tell her how proud
you are. Make sure to keep your excitement all about your child's accomplishment and not about what it means for you.

First Steps

Role Modeling

The number one way any child learns anything is by watching their parent. This is true with kids of every temperament. Goal–Directed Children
seldom need more than encouragement to get them to try something.
They like the feeling of accomplishment and they usually aim to please
their parents. That's not to say they don't ever act out, but in general they
are relatively easy to influence.

Learning good toileting procedures starts long before your child ever
sits on the potty. From the time your child is able to follow you into the
bathroom, you should talk to him about what you're doing in there. Teach

him the proper words for body parts, explain what pee-pee and poop are, show him what happens when you flush, and help him understand this is something he will someday also do on the potty. Answer his questions about it truthfully and as fully as you feel necessary for his particular age.

Potty Talk

Child: Daddy, what are you doing?

Dad: I'm going pee-pee, buddy.

Child: Why?

Dad: Well, I drank a lot of water today, and after my body takes all the good vitamins and minerals out, the rest of the water comes out of my body as pee-pee. I make sure it goes in the potty and then I flush it away, like this. (Flushes) And now I wash my hands.

Child: (watching the flush intently) Where does it go?

Dad: It goes down the drain and, look, now the potty is clean for the next person who has to use it.

If he continues to ask questions, answer as simply and directly as you can. Stay mindful of the fact that some kids are scared of the toilet at first and your answers to their questions are going to either confirm or deny their fears. At this early juncture, you don't need to get into the hygiene aspects of poop and pee-pee being full of germs or the vast system of sewer pipes under the whole town. If you sense he is getting worked up, either because of his imaginative questions or from an accidentally scary answer, gently steer him in another direction for the time being until you can gather your thoughts for a follow-up conversation.

If she is interested, let her sit on the potty and experience what it feels like. There is no reason a child can't sit on the potty long before actual toilet training begins, as long as she isn't forced to do it. If she enjoys feeling like a big kid, by all means, let her get used to spending time there. Start offering up Practice Sessions, as described in Chapter 3. The earlier she comes to think of going potty as a natural part of everyone's routine, the earlier she may decide it also applies to herself, and potentially initiate potty training on her own. You can start her sitting in clothes or not, however she wants to do it. If she likes it, but is still too young to actually train, get her a potty chair of her own and place it right next to the toilet for her to sit on while you're going on the real thing.

Keep some books nearby so she can have something else to do while she sits. If she does this unclothed, you may get some early successes to build on for when you start training in earnest. Praise her often for simply sitting. If she does happen to go pee or poop into the potty, act surprised and happy, but don't overdo it. Make sure any feedback you give is about whatever she accomplished, not about how happy this may make you.

> *Mom: Sweetie, it looks like you've got some pee-pee in the potty there. Did you feel it come out of you? Wow, you're getting to be such a big girl, already going pee-pee on the potty. Way to go! Here, let me show you how to wipe yourself with the toilet paper.*

But if your son or daughter isn't all that curious about what you do when you're sitting on the toilet and doesn't ask to give it a try, don't push it. For whatever reason, she/he isn't yet ready. Continue to model behavior and talk about what you're doing, but don't worry about relating it directly to your child. She/he will figure it out and get interested soon enough. In the meantime, this could be an opportunity to try stage-setting props like books, dolls, and/or videos about toileting.

Scheduling

Before you begin training in earnest, try to observe whether your son or daughter is on any kind of regular elimination schedule. As we suggested in Chapter 3, Universal Strategies, many kids' bodies do start to regulate themselves and that can assist you in your efforts. Watch to see about what time of day your child poops, and try to closely monitor for when the diaper becomes wet—instead of opening them up all the time, you can simply push a little bit on the front or bottom of the diaper often throughout the day; it usually makes a crinkly sound when it's dry. In addition, using a less-absorbent brand may help to determine how often they are wet.

Having a clue of when their body needs to go can be used to schedule sessions of sitting on the potty. This is a method that works very well with Goal-Directed Children, because they understand its value in helping them reach their goal.

The Hop on the Pot idea is this: every half-hour or so throughout the day, sit your child on the potty for a few minutes and give them the opportunity to go. You can use the toilet or a potty chair in the bathroom next to the real thing. In the beginning, it'll be a lot of nothing. Don't make a big deal of whether they actually make any pee or poop. The point right now is to sit. Parents should think of this time as practice for the real thing—the first in a line of many steps toward being trained.

The skills these Practice Sessions teach include learning to sit on cue, to raise and lower pants, and to wash their hands afterward. All of these are important components in using the potty properly. Regardless of whether anything actually comes out, building and practicing these other skills are important parts of the hierarchy and sequence of toileting. Use the Act Like a Coach technique to inspire her to continue to try. Don't let yourself or your child fall into the trap of feeling like the sitting sessions are wasted time. Remember, you can give your child positive reinforcement on any of these related abilities to keep momentum going through the dry spells.

Dad: You are really doing a great job of practicing how to sit on the potty. I'm really glad that when I ask you to, you go right over to the potty and try! You are getting to be such a big boy/girl. I am so proud of you!

This kind of dialog places the emphasis on the child's compliance with the parent's direction and on the stated desired behavior as opposed to the ultimate goal of successfully using the potty. Another way of looking at this is that sitting on the potty is a close approximation of the ultimate desired behavior. By reinforcing closer and closer approximations of the ultimate desired behavior, we shape the child's behavior in a manner that brings it closer to what we eventually want. So by praising your child for how well he's learned to pull down his pants, and then for his patience at sitting on the potty, and finally the way he attempts to push out some pee-pee or poop, you'll be helping him come ever closer to the main goal, which is actually peeing or pooping into the potty.

If sitting becomes monotonous, bring some books into the bathroom with you; even a lap desk with some paper and crayons may be helpful. If it becomes a bit boring, you can start to explain to your Goal-Directed Kid that each time they sit they are making progress toward learning how to go potty like a big kid. Try very hard to plan these practice sessions for when your child is more likely to need to go. You can give them a cup of water to drink to help fill up their bladder.

The first success will probably come because you caught them at the right time. But as soon as they get a taste of that accomplishment, and the proper positive reinforcement from you that will follow, they will be off and running. Talk to them about what they will feel and the muscles they will use. Prepare them for an eventual accident; let them know it happens to everyone when they're learning and that it's okay. Explain about pooping on the potty and how they'll have to learn to wipe themselves but that you'll help them. Make this potty practice a part of your day, just like brushing teeth and taking a bath. If you're not at home with them all day, start this on a weekend or extended vacation and see whether your childcare provider can continue it, even in an amended way. If not, gauge your progress in the time you have and then pick it back up again during the next time period you can.

Use of Deadlines

With most children, the high expectations that accompany a deadline can be too much pressure on their little shoulders. They may freeze up, feel the goal is too far out of reach, and decide it's not even worth attempting. Goal-Directed Children may not react quite as badly to a timetable as their peers. As long as it's kept fairly loose and long-term, you can sensitively clue them in to your timetable and use it as more of an incentive. These kids are usually very eager to learn and quickly become invested in the project.

A long-term goal for the Goal-Directed Child, such as telling them at their third birthday that they can be potty trained by their fourth birthday, may get them really excited. Another example: let's say your daughter or son started asking to learn karate but the school requires all students to be potty trained. You can be honest and discuss the prerequisite with them.

Mom: I think karate would be a terrific thing for you to learn, but they don't allow diapers at the karate school. Tell you what. Let's start learning how to go pee-pee and poop on the potty, and when you are wearing underpants every day we can go and sign you up for karate. The next class starts in six weeks, so let's start learning today! I'll help you.

By Acting Like a Coach and having a specific goal tied to it, you can kick start his or her interest within a certain timetable. Do make sure she/he understands that it'll be okay if she/he doesn't make that short six-week timetable. There will be plenty of chances with other karate classes later on. Make sure you don't break your word—when they reach the goal of wearing underpants every day, sign them up for the class.

If you have a hard-and-fast timetable, such as starting preschool on a specific date, you may want to consider creating an artificial deadline much earlier and working toward that one first. That way, you will have another chance without serious scheduling or financial consequences.

This kind of strategy is specific to the Goal-Directed Child. We suggest skipping a deadline-based incentive if your child exhibits traits from the other personality types. Kids who have secondary Sensory-Oriented or Internalizing tendencies will likely feel too pressured or anxious to be able to comfortably make the deadline. Those with a Strong-Will are apt to see this as a bit of manipulation and thus rebel. Impulsive Children may initially go gangbusters on the potty, but then quickly lose interest and won't understand when they don't get to go to the class.

Nakedtime

As outlined in Chapter 3, nakedtime is a fantastic tool to let your child see and feel the physical aspects of elimination. There is not a whole lot of the technique that needs to be tailored specifically to a Goal-Directed

Kid, so if this is the avenue you choose, you can follow the directions on pages 54-61.

Intensive Training Sessions

With Goal-Directed Boys and Girls, who typically have a short learning curve and don't take offense to your intensive training efforts, it's perfectly permissible to combine our strategies for use all at once. By layering many techniques together, it is conceivable your Goal-Directed Child could be potty trained in one day. For many kids, though, even the most Goal-Directed ones, a single day is probably pushing it; a weekend or a week is more reasonable. Usually, the goal of this kind of rigorous training is to master control over the bladder. If the issue of poop comes up (or out!), by all means tackle it, but for general purposes this will be pee-pee training.

First, you want to be sure your child is actually Goal-Directed. As we mentioned (and explain more later in this chapter), some children masquerade as Goal-Directed but in truth they aren't. Additionally, many parents wish their kids were Goal-Directed, but, again, in reality, they aren't. If your child has characteristics of another personality type, you'll need to take that into consideration and perhaps not attempt this kind of intensive training. In addition, you want to be absolutely positive your child is physically, cognitively, and emotionally ready to potty train. We outline all these indicators in Chapter 2, and perhaps it's worth a reread.

Second, decide which of the training techniques you think will put your child's best foot forward. Hopefully, you have already been role modeling good bathroom habits. Perhaps by now you have the children's books about going potty or have play-acted with a doll. If not, it'll be a good idea to prepare for an intensive training session with these kinds of items.

Third, use the Acting Like a Coach and Give Good Directions techniques to explain to your child what's about to happen. If you are ambitious and trying to do it all in one day, make it a point to talk about it during the previous week, create anticipation, answer questions, ease any fears, and approach it with a sense of big adventure. If you're planning for a weekend or a full week, you should still build up excitement in advance. Prepare yourself as well; clear your schedule of anything else so you can devote 100% of your time to the task at hand.

Fourth, a warning: if at any time your child balks at the idea or practice of this intensive training, back off and realize it's probably going to take him or her a little bit longer to get toileting behavior down pat. And that needs to be okay with you.

So, on P-Day (Potty Day), we think it makes a lot of sense to set aside most of the morning for nakedtime. Your son or daughter should already be able to pull his or her pants on and off, so for now you want to concentrate all efforts on getting the pee-pee and maybe even some poop into the toilet or potty chair. Start early—that means waking up before she/he does and getting his/her diaper off before the day's first pee. If you can get that one into the potty, you will be able to start this momentous day with a success!

Wake him/her up gently, but excitedly, and lead him/her immediately into the bathroom for the ceremonious removal of the diaper. If you've missed the window of opportunity for that first pee, don't let your disappointment show. Instead, lather on the praise for a wonderful first attempt and then steer your child into the area you've chosen for nakedtime.

With such a concentrated schedule, you're going to need to pack in as many potty-related activities as possible. Have all your props in the nakedtime area, ready to go. Give your child an extra cup of water at breakfast, lunch, and dinner, and then whenever she/he asks for more. Layer in some scheduled sitting sessions, and watch your child like a hawk for any indication of the need to eliminate. Bring your child with you when you have to go, and engage in some intensive role modeling at this time. If you've been squeamish in the past about allowing your child an up-close look at your body or your waste products, now's the time to get over it. It's fine to explain to your child that usually people want to have privacy in the bathroom, but your child is really going to need to watch you go today.

Dad: Whoa, I drank a lot of water this morning. Look at how much pee-pee is coming out of me! You know, I don't usually like people to look at my penis and my body this closely; grown-ups like to go to the bathroom in private.

But today is a special Potty Day and so you get to see everything and ask any question you want. After today (or this weekend/this week), though, I'm going to want to go potty by myself, but by then you'll have learned how to do it by yourself! And you can always ask me any question you have.

Build on each small success—recognizing the feelings, telling you they have to go, running really fast to the potty, wiping themselves, washing hands afterward, and of course actually getting the pee-pee or poop into the potty. Study in advance the kind of praise he likes best and then give plenty of it! If he enjoys crowing about success, perhaps you could phone Grandma and tell her how great it's going! If he likes it when you get really excited, come up with a silly Potty Song & Dance to do each time he's triumphant. (Think of football end zone dances and you'll get the idea.) Making up the song and dance could be a great bonding activity for you guys to do in between sit sessions. If he prefers more subdued reactions, you could write down each success and show the list to the rest of the family. The point is to build up their confidence, reinforce their good behavior, and spur them on to the larger goal of bodily control.

Accidents are going to happen, today, and for a while afterward. We don't know of any child who goes from zero to total control over their elimination functions in one day. Some kids who were the easiest to train still have accidents even a year later, albeit usually few and far between. Your reaction to an accident during this intensive training should be matter of fact. You don't want your child to dwell on the failure, you want them to learn from it and move on to what's sure to be a successful next time.

Mom: Okay, babe, this is one accident, but you've done really great trying three times now. Don't worry about it. Next time, just remember that when you feel like the pee-pee is going to come out, you have to stop playing and get to the potty as quick as you can—even if you're playing your favorite game. So, let's just clean you right up, easy as pie, and next time I know you'll do great.

In the middle of this intensive training, you'll want to evaluate how it's going and whether you'll need more time. Many children will, and you shouldn't see this as a failure. If your son or daughter has had a number of successes, this could be a good time to add underwear to the mix and see how she/he does when she/he has to pull them down before going potty. A special surprise might be to have some of your child's favorite character undies on hand to offer. After you feel like she/he has a handle on that, add in pants and other items of clothing, and work up to being fully clothed. You might even make a game out of it by continuing to change his or her outfit (pants, shorts, overalls, dress, tights, shoes, or boots) and see how well they get out of it. Continue with the books, dolls, and modeling behavior.

By the end of the day, weekend, or week, you should see some major progress. Take stock of what your child has learned. As long as they've gotten a tentative hold on the process, it should be underwear from now on. Try not to have too many activities beyond home and daycare for the next few days, so you can alleviate as many accidents as possible. There will be more accidents, but resist the temptation to slide back into diapers.

If your daughter or son is in daycare, it is essential you talk with the teacher about your child's particular schedule and any special treatment they might need while the skills are still new. They've probably seen it before and may even be able to give you some constructive feedback on how she/he is doing.

Handle bowel movements as they come along, and react to poopy accidents the same way as pee-pee. Nighttime dryness should be left for later; we suggest you wait until the daytime behavior is firmly established as a routine. Wiping effectively—both pee and poop—will also take a while, so plan on being on hand to help your child with these skills.

Accidents

Regardless of whether you attempt an intensive training session or not, accidents happen with every child. As long as your child seems willing to continue to use the potty, you can do damage control to make sure she/he doesn't feel overly guilty or like a failure after the inevitable accident. Instead, kids can assist you with the clean up and move forward. Continued accidents may mean the child has achieved skill development but not skill maintenance. If you suspect this is the case, revisit how well you are doing in reinforcing a job well done even after your child has demonstrated a string of successes. Because Goal-Directed Kids can seem a little lower maintenance (they have that internal sense of wanting to accomplish things), parents might too quickly assume that their Goal-Directed Child is finished potty training before the process is actually done. We always run the risk of not noticing when our kids are doing exactly the things we want them to do, and the risk for taking good behavior for granted is particularly high with Goal-Directed Kids.

If accidents start to take over, there may be something else going on and parents should observe closely to see if their child is ill or whether there is an outside influence affecting the potty-training process. A secondary personality trait, such as sensitivity or intensity, might be showing itself, in which case you can try some of the other tactics in the book. For Goal-Directed Children, a potential pitfall is that they interpret the accident as a failure that they then Internalize. If this is the case, back off a little and read Chapter 6.

Proper Identification

As we mentioned earlier in the chapter, some children masquerade as Goal-Directed Children. Other times, it's parents who treat their Sensory-Oriented or Impulsive Child as if they are Goal-Directed. Figuring out the best positive reinforcer for your child's true personality is the key to more effective parenting and teaching, whether it's about going in the potty, or later on about something else, such as homework habits. So if your child doesn't take to a simple rewards' system readily, take a good long look at the descriptions in the other chapters, and see if perhaps there are some other personality traits that may help identify another, more suitable training technique.

Goal-Directed Children often like to be independent, and it may throw off the balance a little when their parents get overly involved. If they feel as though achieving potty training is not their own goal, they may not engage very well. They may not like to feel manipulated or coerced into doing something they don't really want to do. This does not mean they are Strong-Willed, although that trait could be lurking in their subconscious. Rather, it emphasizes their desire for independence, which is a very positive trait in most kids and should be fostered so they will carry it with them into their school years.

•••

Now that you have a better understanding of the temperament of a Goal-Directed Child, as well as the techniques that may spur his acquisition of potty-training skills, you can start to plan your approach. From setting the stage to determining proper reinforcement of good potty behavior, you can begin this process.

But, as stated in the final section, many Goal-Directed Children have strong secondary personality traits or are masquerading as a Goal-Directed temperament. Therefore, we advise all parents to read through the entirety of this book to get a handle on the full range of issues that can affect potty training both positively and negatively. Being fully informed will help you counter any potential challenge that pops up, as well as allow you to understand why other children in your playgroup or your kids' cousins trained in such a different manner than yours. This perspective can be extraordinarily valuable, especially for parents who plan on having more children.

5

The Sensory-
Oriented Child

The Sensory-Oriented Child is one who has a distinct comfort zone relating to each of their senses. Each person has their own sensory threshold—all of us at some point will complain that something is too loud, too hard, too smelly, too painful, etc. The "normal" reaction to a stimulus is defined by the majority of people's reactions, but we all have our breaking points. Sensory-Oriented Kids just have a lower threshold, thus they tend to find stimuli in the "normal" range more noxious than the rest of us. Therefore, they seemingly overreact to things that are outside the comfort zone they've established for themselves.

In this chapter, you will learn about this temperament, and how to think about the long-term benefits to a careful approach to potty training. Along with specific ways to alleviate those challenges that often make potty training difficult for kids with sensory issues, we'll give you tips and techniques on easing into the process, ways to decrease their discomfort, and how separating the skills of going pee and going poop can be helpful.

The Sensory-Oriented Temperament

Sensory-Oriented Kids show an exaggerated response to noises that are considered normal by other people. Loud music or a vacuum cleaner, even the applause of a crowd, will be too strident, although it may not seem out of proportion to the rest of us, and they may quickly cover their ears.

They are often very sensitive about textures of clothing. They complain about being bothered by tags, find everything itchy, and are always either too warm or too cold. Parents find themselves smoothing out the toe of every sock or risk having shoes pulled off a hundred times before their child says it feels "right." You can forget about putting him or her in anything remotely fancy. Another telltale sign your toddler or preschooler is Sensory-Oriented is that when you finally find a shirt she/he likes to wear without complaint, you buy one in every color available, sometimes even more in the next size up.

Sensory-Oriented Children are also overly aware of smells and tastes. They tend to be nonadventurous and very picky eaters. They usually decide that they don't like a new food before they have ever tried it. (Okay, we know most kids say this occasionally, but with Sensory-Oriented Children it's a constant refrain.) They may also smell things from a mile away or simply react with quick irritation at any excessively enveloping odor. It's not that they just don't like the smell, but the pervasiveness of it through a room could even make them feel physically ill.

If your son or daughter falls within this personality type, he/she likely will startle very easily and can be difficult to comfort once upset. These children exaggerate minor bumps and bruises and they usually require "treatments" such as a kiss before moving on, or a bandage where there is no real scrape. They have a tendency to overfocus on anything that might cause them discomfort, and it can be difficult to talk them through their fear when they are upset. They get wrapped up in it and close themselves off to your attempts to calm them. These children are apt to be relatively intense in terms of their emotional reactions to things, and their emotions tend toward the anxious side.

It may seem as if they are scared by everything overloading their senses, but if you look a little more closely, you might be able to tell, for example with something that's too loud, whether it is fear of the noise or the volume of the noise that is adversely affecting them. This is one way to differentiate between a Sensory-Oriented Child and an Internalizer. The Internalizer might be frightened by the noise, or think that it represents a threat to them, whereas the Sensory-Oriented Kid simply recoils from the noxiousness of the stimulus and may not necessarily express fear. However, the Sensory-Oriented Child may quickly develop fears based on the adverse reaction she/he anticipates and associates with these stimuli.

In addition, the Sensory-Oriented Child has a propensity to be cautious in new situations and withdraw from novelty. As long as they are well within their comfort zone, they will demonstrate a lot of the positive traits associated with any child. When comfortable, they may not be easy to distinguish from another personality type. However, they are very easily distracted by anything that might provoke physical irritation. These children often feel like they are out of control and at the mercy of their environment. To put it a bit differently, these children often feel as though at any minute another loud noise, or other noxious stimulus, could occur and scare or hurt them.

Parents of Sensory-Oriented Sons and Daughters know their children can be very difficult to accommodate, particularly with things like food and clothing choices. These kids are likely to be relatively shy with new people and are slow to warm up to anyone or anything because they are trying to limit the number of things that take them out of their established comfort zone. At other times, when their reactions to sensitivities take over, they shut down, and often must cycle through the full range of a meltdown before they can be calmed. These outbursts can be similar to a temper tantrum, but the origin of them is a bit different than simply getting mad when things don't go their way. Parents of Sensory-Oriented Children often find they inadvertently adapt to their kids without even realizing it; their world revolves around their child's sensitivities. It's easy to fall into a pattern of only offering foods the child enjoys, shopping for hours to find the right clothing, offering endless choices, and being willing to change things around in order to meet the child's every sensitivity whim. We don't fault you for it—avoiding those meltdowns and endless readjustments are a priority for your happy family life. But, now, with potty training on the horizon, your child's sensitivities are about to take over even more than they may have in the past, so starting off on the right foot is critical.

These children are susceptible to plenty of toileting difficulties partly as a result of their sensory issues. Sensory-Oriented Kids may feel the potty is too cold, hate the flushing sound, or be frightened when the water splashes up. They may feel unstable on the toilet seat especially if their feet are not touching the ground, they may not like the excess of smells involved in the process, and will have issues with the mess of accidents. As a result, some of their toileting difficulty may come from their need to have some control in a world that they otherwise feel is completely random and frightening to them.

Thinking Long Term

Plan for a long haul in training your Sensory-Oriented Son or Daughter. It may take some time for him or her to become accustomed to everything involved and to overcome the anxieties. The thoughtful parent of a Sensory-Oriented Child will understand that easing into each part of the process is what will facilitate long-term success. Just like people of every temperament, these kids need to have ownership of the goal on their terms.

Parents need to learn to allow their kids to retain control over their own bodily functions. You may have already run into trouble with sleeping or feeding your Sensory-Oriented Child. Remember, no human being can compel another to eat, sleep, or go to the bathroom.

Just because your child has exaggerated sensitivities does not mean you need to force him or her to become desensitized. It's a myth to think that if you continually expose your child to the things he or she is scared of, eventually he or she won't be scared of them anymore—for example, having the child stay in the bathroom to hear the toilet flush a hundred times until they can "tolerate" the sound. One of the things you really want to avoid with this type of child is crossing the threshold into provoking fear and anxiety and sensory overload. Once a Sensory-Oriented Kid crosses that line, she/he is usually responding on raw emotion and the episode turns negative. This can create later problems because the child may associate strong negative feelings (and that visceral fear feeling) with attempts at potty training. Along the same lines, these kids quickly learn to connect new things with fear and anxiety and overload. Parents need to keep in mind that their calm, sometimes cautious, and muted reactions are what's best for these children.

Empathizing with their sensitive state of mind, even if you don't completely understand the triggers, will help your children progress. Acknowledge their concerns and help them work through it. Give them the compassion they need and assure them you will be right there beside them, safeguarding them. Build in some breaks to the training process, time to become acclimated to the new way of doing things, and also time to become confident in their newfound skill before tackling another. Slowly, they will enlarge their comfort zone and allow going on the potty to become an established part of their lives. In the meantime, you'll need to let them progress at their own pace.

Ease Into It

Much like swimming or bathing in cool water, your Sensory-Oriented Son or Daughter will want to test the temperature first with just the toes, dangling them until they adjust to the coolness. Then they dip their feet in, again waiting until they're used to the temperature before going in further. In the same way—slowly, carefully, warily—they'll test the waters of potty training. They won't advance to the next step until they've become accustomed to the current one.

Plan to ease into potty training slowly and subtly, such that they won't notice anything is different at first. As with other personality types, the bigger the deal you make of training, the more put off your Sensory-Oriented Child may become. So, simply don't say much about it directly. Just because this is a huge undertaking you've been thinking (dreaming!) about for a long time doesn't mean it needs to be one more in a long line of important concerns for your child. He or she probably has enough concerns, and will certainly sense your expectations, and so the very first forays into potty training should be small.

Modeling the behavior yourself is always the best way to begin. Children of any mindset learn primarily from watching and imitating their parents. Start by having them in the bathroom with you and talking about what you're doing. Narrate your actions out loud, but don't direct them at your child. Just simply state what you are doing when you are doing it. If this makes you uncomfortable, ask your spouse to do it.

Mom: Hi sweetie. I just need to go pee-pee and then we can play that game together. I'm just going to sit, push the pee-pee out—can you hear it?—wipe, and then flush. Now, I've got to wash my hands, because we always wash our hands after going to the bathroom, and then I'm done. Now, where's that game?

After a few times, make a casual remark that maybe they'll want to try sitting on the potty one day.

Mom: . . . and then we flush. Maybe someday you'll want to try it, too. It doesn't have to be today, but someday, if you want to, it'd be okay.

Your Sensory-Oriented Child may or may not be interested at this point. Take their cue and follow it. If they want, let them sit on the potty. Many Sensory-Oriented Children will only want to do this wearing clothes at first. They will want a layer between their skin and the potty. They may hop on for a split second and then jump right off again. Regardless, praise them for trying. If they seem a little unnerved by the experience, tell them how proud you are of them. Don't heap it on too strong, just a statement of congratulations and then move on to whatever activity is planned.

Dad: Wow, you did it! You sat on the potty! I'm proud of you, buddy. If you ever want to try it again, just let me know and I'll help you.

Now, this may seem like a very open-ended option, and to their ears that's exactly how it should sound. You, however, will be setting the stage, so to speak, so that their interest in using the potty will grow. Continue to narrate your actions in the bathroom, even the ones peripheral to potty training. In fact, this is a great tool to use to teach any kind of proper behavior. Make it a point to tell your child when you are using the toilet before an activity or outing, and explain why. Mention the times when you have to go, but have to wait until you can get to a bathroom. A great way to do this is in the car when you're almost at home—strapped in their car seat, your child is a "captive" listener and will be anticipating your arrival at home. Describe what it feels like when your bladder is full, and explain to them how you are using your muscles to keep the pee-pee in until you can get home and get to the toilet. If you're an enterprising actor, you might even do a little bit of the "gotta-go dance"—something like that is certain to get your kid's attention! When you do get home, be obvious about making a beeline for the potty before doing anything else. Your child will notice and may actually follow you into the bathroom, at which point you can continue to discuss what you're doing and why.

Mom: Oh boy, am I glad we made it home quick. I really had to go pee-pee. I was holding it tight inside my body when we were in the car, but I could feel it needed to come out. Phew, I feel better now that I've been able to go on the potty. I'm just going to wash my hands and then let's go and get all our stuff out of the car.

This also might be a good opportunity to bring up the possibility of an accident; again, relate it only to you.

Mom: You know, when I was a little girl learning how to go pee-pee and poop on the potty, I had some accidents and sometimes it came out before I was ready. But it was okay. That happens to everyone. My mommy—Grandma—just helped clean me up, and pretty soon I learned how to hold it.

What you are in effect doing is heading the fears off at the pass, as much as that is possible. By discussing the kind of thing they might be anxious about before it even happens to them, you'll be taking a preemptive step to alleviate their fears and ease them into potty training.

Resist the urge to compare your Sensory-Oriented Child with your friend's Goal-Directed Child (or any other personality type for that matter). Match ups like that will only frustrate and perhaps instigate you to rush your child beyond their comfort level, which will, in turn, set your timetable back a ways. We know you'll be tempted to push things a little faster, but at these times we urge you to remember your child is governed by his or her personality, and you are using corresponding training techniques in a thoughtful, caring way. The timetable for toilet training must be set by your child and no one else.

Backing Off

Plan to periodically back off throughout the entire process. Try one thing and let them get that down before you rush into another. Feel them out though, don't just assume they are or are not ready. Ask gentle questions about how they're feeling.

Discuss whatever the next step is beforehand, again in a very casual way. Giving them information in advance not only prepares them, but gives them the opportunity to take the initiative to request moving forward or to do it on their own. Remember, for Sensory-Oriented Kids, it's all about their need to feel in control and comfortable.

Creature Comforts

The sensitivities that Sensory-Oriented Children exhibit may not only be a part of their personality; they may actually have sensitive skin. Tags itch, socks bunch, shirtsleeves have to be pulled down all the way underneath jackets, and wool sweaters are out of the question. It may seem imaginary or exaggerated to you, especially if the fabric feels soft to your touch. Because kids of this personality type put so much stock in the way things feel, capitalize on this by having them help you shop for the softest toilet paper. Single rolls aren't that expensive, so buy a couple and do a "softness test" just like in a TV commercial. Not only will this help your child feel in control of a part of this process, she'll get a kick out of seeing those commercials from now on. Use the ones she doesn't pick in your own bathroom, unless of course you or your spouse are also Sensory-Oriented. If your child has concerns about the comfort of the potty, take her with you to pick out a child-sized toilet ring. A character or interesting design will give you the opportunity to approach this with your child as a fun activity. Setting the tone is as important as setting the stage. Pick out the kind of soap you keep in your kid's bathroom in the same way. Washing hands is another big, important skill to learn—and sometimes another struggle for a Sensory-Oriented Child—so pick the kind of soap that smells, feels, and looks nice to them.

Because they are now going to be washing their hands on, we presume, a much more regular basis than before, keep an eye out for itchy, scratchy, dry skin. After all, you don't want to get them potty trained only to have a huge battle over handwashings! Perhaps have some moisturizer available to alleviate the possibility. They may really like the feeling of rubbing the lotion onto their skin and that may even become the most anticipated part of the entire ritual, although it shouldn't be the focus.

We don't mean to say that you should cater to their every whim; there is a fine line between that and setting them up for success at a task like potty training.

First Steps

Role Modeling

If possible, train along gender lines—moms train daughters and fathers train their sons. However, when making these decisions, you absolutely need to factor in the personality types of you and your spouse, or any adult who will be taking a main role in the training. To use a very stereotypical example, a Strong-Willed or Goal-Directed Dad teaching his Sensory-Oriented Son will need to be extra careful to set aside his own personality during this delicate time. If you are unsure whether that will be possible, then training across gender lines will be the better choice (providing, of course, that Mom can either downplay her personality or is also of the Sensory-Oriented type). Whoever is the primary trainer should maintain a relaxed, tranquil attitude about the whole thing.

Practice Sessions

With a Sensory-Oriented Child, Practice Sessions will help you ease into the process. It will also give you clues as to which parts of the process are going to be more difficult for your child. As one of the first steps after you've been Role Modeling potty behavior for a while, you could suggest that your child try to climb up to the toilet or potty, sit on it fully clothed, and go through the motions of pretending to pee or poop: get the toilet paper, wipe, flush, and wash hands. Any red flags with sensory issues there (except for the smells) may make themselves known, giving you an idea of what you're going to need to deal with more carefully.

Use Practice Sessions throughout potty training, practicing the next skill in the process as you and your child move forward. Keep your eyes and ears open for any other red flags, because sometimes they don't present themselves immediately. In this way, you can continue to ease her into the next steps, while building on the successes you've already accomplished.

Nakedtime

As noted in other chapters, most kids relish the opportunity to run around naked, and Sensory-Oriented Children are no different. Toilet training is a perfect opportunity to not only allow but encourage it. Nakedtime is the ultimate way of giving your child control over his or her own potty-training destiny. Basically, the idea is to let your toddler run around naked for certain periods of the day, or all day if you want, and allow nature to take its course. When the inevitable happens, your child will have, for the first time, a clear view of the physical mechanics of going potty. Yes, it can be messy, but if you orchestrate it specifically for easy clean up, nakedtime is a great way to show cause and effect, plus it will naturally direct your son or daughter to the potty.

Again, careful planning is needed to make sure your child is receptive to the idea when you suggest it. Following are some things you need to consider to keep your child comfortable during nakedtime: if outside, you should consider the weather, the privacy of your yard, the ground surfacing, how you'll manage a quick clean up, and any favorite activities (like a slide) that might need to be off limits; if inside, you need to take into account any roaming restrictions you've put in place, and having enough activities within your desired area to keep your child entertained.

At first, start by simply letting him run around naked. As we outlined in the Nakedtime section of Chapter 3, you can optimize this technique by scheduling nakedtime for the part of the day when their bodies are programmed to go. Give them an extra cup of water just before you start, as well, to increase the chances of them needing to pee.

With Sensory-Oriented Kids, as opposed to any of the other temperament categories we outline in this book, you will need to clue them in a bit about what may happen. With other kinds of children, we specif-ically suggest not mentioning the purpose behind nakedtime, but the personality of a Sensory-Oriented Child requires some forewarning about the possibility of an accident.

> *Dad (very upbeat voice): Hey, buckaroo, wanna do something crazy and fun today? How about if I let you run around naked for a little while? I know, we don't usually let you do that, but let's be different today! (After getting clothes off, express this last part subtly) . . . Oh, and bud, listen, because you don't have a diaper on you might have some pee-pee or poop come out of your body, but don't worry, if that happens, we'll clean you right up. Now, let's go!*

Keep it simple and factual. You want to let them know what might happen to head off their fears, but you don't want to create any appre-hension if it's not already there. Then, just watch and wait.

Try to stay near your child during nakedtime, especially the first few sessions, until you can gauge their reaction. When the inevitable happens, respond quickly but calmly. Immediately soothe them and ex-plain what's happening. If they seem scared, tell them there is nothing to be afraid of, that everyone goes pee-pee and poop.

Accidents

Sensory-Oriented Children will react very negatively to accidents, espe-cially if you raise your voice or the mess gets on their legs or clothes. It may be your uncontrollable first reaction to yell to make him stop the pee or poop, but this will only backfire. You may grab your child up and run him into the bathroom to control the mess, but this may likely scare your Sensory-Oriented Child. Be especially careful. Perhaps go back to the quiz section of the book and think about your own personality type. If you tend to be stubborn, and thus want things done your way and to be the one in control all the time, you're going to have to adjust your thinking. It's not easy, but that's why you're the parent. Even if your child poops in the center of your white-carpeted living room, keep an even voice. Gently but quickly steer her to the nearest surface that is more easily cleaned (kitchen, patio, bathroom, even a throw rug). Be positive by explaining that these things happen to everyone. Perhaps you can distract her with a story about how you had a big accident just like this when you were learning how to go potty, but you learned and now you're a grownup who goes in the potty every time. For the first few accidents, continuing quickly on with the fun activities is best. Your goal is to get your Sensory-Oriented Child to turn their dislike of the pee/poop running down their legs into a desire to put it into the potty.

One possible way to make this easier during nakedtime in particular is to have a potty chair available. Again, like the toilet paper, soap, or ring, let your child pick one out that makes them feel comfortable. As with most children, transit time to the toilet is of the essence. The biggest incentive for the Sensory-Oriented Kid will be avoiding the mess. Many Sensory-Oriented Children may have an aversion to the big, high, cold toilet in your bathroom. A potty chair is not only portable, but small, cute, and low enough to make them feel steady with their feet flat on the ground. Using them makes a lot of sense in this situation; the only drawback is that it means an eventual transition to the big toilet. Part of taking this process slowly though is making time for transitions like these, and we believe the benefits will in most cases be worth it. Successfully training your child to use a potty chair, and transitioning them to underwear, will move you forward in the overall goal. These skills are the basis for all the others, and the learning curve gets smaller with each skill acquired.

In rare cases, Sensory-Oriented Children can become concerned for their own safety the first time they have an accident, perhaps thinking they've sprung a "leak" of some kind. The "stuff" is going to be warm and smelly, or even worse, running down their legs, which will be quite repellent. They need that forewarning we suggested earlier. In addition, if you've been modeling bathroom behavior for a while, that may help them to not jump to the wrong conclusion about what's happening. Regardless, you'll have to identify that this is their pee-pee and poop coming out of them, just like what you've been telling them comes out of you in the bathroom.

> ## Potty Talk
>
> **Mom:** (calm, cool, and collected): Okay, sweetie, that's some pee-pee/poop coming out of you. You're okay. Mommy does that too, but I sit on the potty and my pee-pee and poop goes in there. You can do that, too, sometime, if you want.
>
> **Child:** (scared): Mommy!!!
>
> **Mom:** You're okay. Everyone has accidents like this—I did when I was a little girl, and it scared me a little. Do you remember how I told you that happened? Grandma just helped clean me up and then I felt better. I'll help you just like Grandma helped me. Here, let's get that pee-pee/poop off.

Separating the Pee from the Poop

Some kids get peeing down very quickly, but the process stalls when it comes to poop. Obviously, moving your bowels is a much more intense process, at times filled with noxious smells, straining muscles, and splashing water—all anathema to your Sensory-Oriented Child. In your decision making, consider the benefits of splitting your training techniques into two different sections, one for pee and a totally separate one for poop. Increase your use of Practice Sessions each time you get to another major skill. You can, in fact, break up all of the toileting skills into as many separate teachable actions as you need. We also suggest you separate daytime training from nighttime training, for example. The concept is the same with separating the pee from the poop.

Use the above methods to get started with pee-pee, and ignore anything having to do with poop. (Of course, if your child has to go poop during nakedtime—you can't exactly ignore that—just assist in the way that is the easiest and most appropriate, without comment on how it relates to learning how to go pee-pee on the potty.) Focus your teaching energies on supporting your child's efforts to control his or her bladder muscles during the daytime hours. Once he or she is comfortable with peeing in the potty, you can introduce the idea of wearing underpants instead of a diaper.

Sensory-Oriented Kids may have a hard time transitioning from bulky padding around their rear to a slip of cotton that feels like nothing. Starting with training pants that have a little padding down below might be helpful (they also absorb well during accidents). If your child has sensory issues with other articles of clothing, look for brands without tags, and, whenever possible, try them on in the store before buying them. You want your child to be comfortable and enjoy the experience of wearing big girl or big boy undies, and your child should have ownership in this momentous occasion. And, at this point, they may sense just how momentous it is! Don't do this too quickly after you start training, but if a few days of nakedtime, or your chosen technique, yields good results, then go for it. Give your child some "try-on" times to wear the underwear around for fifteen minutes to an hour twice a day before they are expected to wear them for an entire day. Highlight the benefits of the new underwear:

Dad: I think you run faster wearing underwear instead of that bulky diaper— let's time you and see!

Pick a day for "First Day of Underwear" when you don't have to be anywhere and can devote your day to supporting your child's new skills. Be especially watchful to avoid an accident on this day. There might be nothing worse than having your child be so proud to put on the chosen underpants only to quickly wet through them and, by extension, dampen her or his pride. To head off a traumatic experience, prepare your child for the eventuality that they will have an accident in their new underwear, but that you will just wash them like you wash all their clothes and they will become clean again.

The Dirty Diaper

Annabelle is a very stereotypical three-year-old girl. Her favorite game is to pretend she's a Princess. She's got the tulle skirt, kiddie heels, purse, "jewels," and, of course, the tiara in her dress-up trunk.

She even began to insist she be called Belle, just like one of the Disney© characters. So, when it came to picking out her first set of big-girl panties, Annabelle naturally selected the ones with the Disney Princesses printed on them. "She was so proud to be wearing them around," her mother, Jess, reported. "Unfortunately, she had an accident just an hour after putting the first pair on, and was inconsolable for having peed all over her favorite Princess."

Jess and Annabelle's story is quite common. A forewarning will work wonders to help your Sensory-Oriented Son or Daughter through this kind of situation.

------- Training Tip --------------------

If you purchase two packs of the undies, you'll have an understudy Princess, or whatever, ready when needed.

Although a choice of underwear is a good way to start, don't allow your child to later manipulate themselves back into diapers by suddenly deciding the underwear he picked out now doesn't suit him. Listen to his rationale, of course, and if you see any merit in his reasoning, perhaps another shopping trip is in order, but if you sense the change of mind is simply a delay tactic, you may have to make a tough choice about how to move forward. Parents can take comfort in the fact that their Sensory-Oriented Child successfully adapted to undies, even if temporarily. So you have evidence it is not the underpants themselves that led to the child's desire to go back to diapers. Parents of Sensory-Oriented Kids are often used to adapting to their child's requirements, so your initial reaction may be to give in to the request to revert to diapers. Instead, you should consider options that give him the opportunity to "control" his discomfort; for example, offer to let him add fabric softener to the laundry. This way you aren't in the position of ignoring your child's discomfort, rather you're simply not allowing diapers to come back into the equation.

Once your child is safely and irrevocably into their chosen underpants during the day, you'll want to pause a bit in your training. Remember that we told you earlier in this chapter that building in some breaks will be beneficial? Now is one of those times. Resist the urge to move on, for just a little while. It doesn't need to be a lot of time, just enough to build up his or her self-confidence and pride in what she/he has thus far accomplished. Of course, if you feel your son or daughter is raring to go, by all means, press forward. Just make sure it's on your child's terms.

Advanced Skills

When you begin the poop training, you may well feel as if you're back at square one. You're not, of course, but your child may show signs of many of the same kinds of sensory issues as when you were teaching him or her to pee in the potty. The bad odors, more intense sensations, and—let's lay it on the line—sometimes noisy expulsions that go along with moving your bowels, are probably in your Sensory-Oriented Child's Top-Ten List of things to be avoided.

Whereas some Sensory-Oriented Children make the transition to pooping on the potty fairly readily, many will need additional encouragement and training. Depending on their body's rhythm, they may have been simply pooping first thing in the morning while still wearing the diaper from overnight, or they've requested a diaper when they've felt the need to poop. There are both good and bad aspects to either of these scenarios. If they've been pooping first thing in the morning, they most likely haven't yet associated the need to poop with the idea of going on the potty. However, if you've been modeling bathroom behavior for a while, this isn't a likely scenario. They probably already know that poop belongs in the potty to be flushed away, but just haven't wanted to try it out for themselves. The kids who've been requesting diapers are probably advanced enough in their muscular control—they already recognize the signals their body gives when they have to go, and this prompts them to ask for a diaper. What needs to happen for them now is to be weaned off the diaper as the preferred receptacle for elimination.

It's not so easy. Sensory-Oriented Kids, pooping in the potty for the first time, are often shocked to feel water splashing up onto their bottom. This can be the ultimate in revulsion for them, and it may put them off poop training. Our suggestions are to either get out that potty chair again (no water, no splash) or to place a couple of layers of toilet paper into the water before they sit down to poop. The paper will "catch" the poop and limit the splashing. Just take care not to clog the toilet and cause it to overflow, because that will also negatively affect your Sensory-Oriented Child and, quite possibly, your spouse.

Kids with sensory issues may take a good long while to adapt to everything that goes along with pooping in the potty. Some will be anxious about the same thing every time—the splashing, the smells, or whatever particularly gets to your child. Others will fret about one thing one day, another thing the next. Regardless of the pattern of your child's angst, keep your responses calm and matter of fact. Resist getting caught up in the drama, because going in the potty is a natural part of life that will continue. But reacting to your Sensory-Oriented Daughter or Son's worries in a thoughtful, kind way will mean a great deal.

After pooping is added to their potty repertoire, your child will again likely have some more sensory obstacles to hurdle. The more advanced potty skills may continue to give trouble—in particular, perhaps, wiping poop effectively. It's easy to fall into the habit of calling for Mom (okay, sometimes Dad!) to come and do it—better than getting any yucky poop on their hands, that's for sure. In teaching them good hygiene, you've likely given them many reasons to want to avoid wiping themselves. Treat this, or any of the advanced skills that challenge their sensitivities, the same way you treated the earlier skills: take it slow, try to understand their fears, and then work together to alleviate them.

Nighttime dryness tactics aren't really any different from what's recommended in Chapter 3's Universal Strategies. Your child's sensitivities may be intensified by waking up to a wet bed, so the sheet/mattress pad layering technique will be something you should do. Continue to use positive reinforcement, and remember it's perfectly fine to wait until you notice dry diapers in the mornings and it all happens naturally.

•••

In this chapter, we delved into the psyche of your Sensory-Oriented Child so we can better understand why they have a lower threshold for stimuli that the rest of us. The five senses, especially touch, smell, and hearing, are more sensitive and produce exaggerated responses from your child.

By easing into potty training, periodically backing off when she needs a break, and breaking down the process using Practice Sessions you can help your child be successful. It bears repeating that you should plan for the long haul with your Sensory-Oriented Child, but the thoughtfulness and caring you take now will reap dividends when training goes smoothly, no matter how slowly.

6

The Internalizer

Internalizers are the kinds of people who, even at young ages, must think everything through. They pride themselves on careful consideration of every angle of a situation. An Internalizer does not attempt a task until she feels she can do it perfectly. She is serious, cautious, and perhaps less active than other types of children. The four walls of your home are likely her comfort zone, in which she will be happy, well-adjusted, and outgoing. Beyond those walls, your kid might seem anxious or guarded. She may privately or quietly rehearse a skill while she is learning it.

In this chapter, we will not only give you a peek inside the mind of an Internalizer, but also explain why you must take some pretraining steps with this type of child. These include bringing the bathroom and toilet-related items and activities into your child's consciousness, into his circle of trust. We will also go through those Universal Strategies that especially resonate with an Internalizer.

The Internalizing Temperament

Internalizing Children are not necessarily timid, but wary, conservative, and prudent. In past generations, Internalizers might have been labeled "fraidy-cats" because their fears are easily provoked. They are apprehensive when trying something for the first time. They may in fact defer that first try for quite a while. Take, for example, sliding down the "big" slide at the playground. An Internalizer may be very obvious in his desire to try it, but despite your assurances that you'll catch him at the bottom, he may simply prefer to watch the other kids slide. He may stand there watching for a long time, seemingly passive. What he is really doing is closely observing the other kids' movements, conducting surveillance on their techniques, and computing the risk of a fall. He mentally puts himself in the other child's place, deciding how he will sit down, push off, and land. All kids do this to an extent, but the Internalizer takes a particularly long amount of time in study.

Of course, this meticulous scrutiny of the behavior of others will bring many benefits as your child matures into an adult. He may be very perceptive and able to read body language well. He shows careful forethought and calculates risk before taking action (you'll love that come the teen years!). He typically concentrates when in pursuit of a goal, once he decides it's a wise course of action, and so he will likely have a good work ethic in school and during his career.

Internalizing Toddlers and Preschoolers are slow to adapt to new situations and prefer close proximity to a parent at all times. Your child is not the type to go off exploring on his or her own. In fact, you may never have seen the need to baby-proof your house. If you are baffled by how your friends have to lock up every cabinet and keep their kids corralled into certain rooms of the house, you likely have an Internalizer on your hands. Many parents actually find themselves trying to encourage these kinds of kids to take a risk on something!

Typically happy within a comfort zone, your son or daughter is earnest in every activity. She/he is intense and resolute, even when coloring or sculpting clay. She/he is a self-focused thinker, ruminating on an issue to figure out how it will affect his or her life. Such egocentric behavior is very common with toddlers and preschoolers of any personality type, but you'll see an Internalizer linger on past experiences a while longer than others.

Breaking through the barriers put up by your Internalizer will be the potty-training challenge. These children may prefer to continue to wear a diaper long after they have the physical ability to go on the toilet, simply because it is what is familiar to them. They may have a tendency to go off by themselves to have a bowel movement, and afterward be quick to tell you that they need a change. However, even if asked beforehand if they need to use the bathroom, they will not admit to it.

Pretraining Steps

Offering toileting information early and often to your child to increase knowledge and encourage interest is a good beginning, but from there we suggest a series of presteps every parent of an Internalizing Child should take. These are not potty-training tactics, per se, as they will not teach your child how to go in the potty. Instead, these are small, virtually unnoticeable changes to your routine that will alleviate or negate certain foreseeable anxieties.

First, starting today, change all diapers in the bathroom. Do it on the floor if necessary; a bathmat makes a fine location. We know one parent whose laundry was in the downstairs bathroom, so she made a changing table out of the top of the dryer. Hey, it was always warm! The reason the location is so important is that this will familiarize your child with that room. Being in there later on will not be a big deal, so one hurdle in the future potty training will be flattened. Your child will automatically connect elimination with the bathroom.

Second, begin to empty poop from the diapers into the toilet and flush it away. This doesn't have to be immediate, but should start around the time your child is learning his "potty words." Allow, but don't force, him to observe. If you just start doing it, he'll notice; you probably won't even have to call it to his attention. The association of poop, potty, and flush will reduce the anxiety that is sure to crop up later on. Thus, another hurdle is avoided.

Modeling bathroom behavior is the best strategy to take with any child, but it is extraordinarily important to your little Internalizer. Remember, she watches others closely before she will take any action herself, and so you need to give her the opportunity to do so with you—the biggest influence in her life.

As explained in Chapter 3, Universal Strategies, keep it natural and easygoing. Most kids at this age will follow you into the bathroom when you have to go, especially Internalizers, who like to stay close by. Begin to use potty breaks as teachable moments, and talk about what you are doing in there. The aim is to familiarize your child with the words, concepts, equipment, sounds, smells, and actions of peeing and pooping. If all of this is known, their concerns about attempting the feat themselves will be lessened. If they have months or years to observe you in action, it may very well be that they decide going on the potty is a goal they want to achieve and virtually potty train themselves. In this way, it might be possible to see your Internalizer morph into a Goal-Directed Child, but if that happens, it needs to be 100% on his or her own terms.

When you're going to the bathroom, explain to your child what you're doing. Put your actions into words. There is no need, at this point, to relate anything you are doing to the fact that he or she will someday be expected to do the same thing. It may feel absurd to say all of this out loud, but we guarantee it will benefit your child. Keep it simple, almost like a child's storybook.

> *Mom: Okay, here we are in the bathroom. I'm going to go potty. I pull down my pants and underwear, and then I sit down. Hmm . . . gotta wait for a few seconds until the pee-pee comes out—oh, here it is! Is it all out? Yup! Okay, do I have to go poop right now? I think I'll push for just a second and see . . . nope! So, I'll just wipe myself with the toilet paper, pull up my pants, and flush. Bye-bye, pee-pee!*

Like the little sponges they are, your children will take the information you give and—as they are aptly named—internalize it to process later. Provide as many details as you feel comfortable with, and then consider giving even more. Internalizers typically need more information than other children do. Observing and having explanations for this behavior allows them to mentally go through it, which is less threatening than actually doing it themselves. Think of it like a virtual experience or simulation. Ask yourself if you would prefer jumping out of a virtual airplane before you'd even consider skydiving. To your child, going on the potty is no less intimidating, unless she/he is frequently exposed to it.

You can talk about any aspect of potty training in this manner—recognizing the signs of having to go, holding it until you can get to the bathroom, pooping, washing hands, etc. Everything you discuss will make its way into your child's subconscious.

When you're ready to start—or more importantly when your child is ready—ask him to participate in small ways with this process. Begin with the most nonthreatening invitation for him to "say bye-bye" to the pee-pee and poop, too. If he complies, inquire if he'd like to pull the handle and flush it away. Many toddlers can't physically pull the lever down, but most are excited to try. Make this game into a ritual for your child, ask your spouse to do the same, and you'll soar over the common hurdle of fear of flushing.

There is no such thing as too much information for an Internalizer, as long as she is requesting intellectual knowledge about the process. Be sure to read and analyze her cues, however. If you notice that the questions tend to focus on one particular aspect of the process, you should consider whether your answers are playing up fears more than contributing necessary information. If you suspect this is the case, you should immediately try to head off her anxieties.

Potty Talk

Dad: Whoa, bud, you're asking a whole lot of questions about poop. Are you worried about having to poop on the potty someday?

Dad: (regardless of child's answer): It's okay. Mom and I know it might be a little scary for you. We were a little scared ourselves when we were learning—everyone is. Don't worry; you don't have to try to poop on the potty until you're ready. When you do try, we'll be right here to help you, and I think you'll see it's pretty easy.

Try to keep your potty-training hopes, dreams, and expectations under wraps. Nothing kills a kid's natural interest like parental pressure.

Your Internalizing Son or Daughter will already have built up quite a bit of stress on their own; they certainly don't need more from you. The thoughtful, careful parent will understand this. If you use the Act Like a Coach technique, you need to be a very quiet, noncompetitive type of coach. You should be vigilant about watching your words, reactions, and timing, despite your yearning for a diaper-free child.

We urge all parents to examine their own personality while they are examining their child's, and consider the compatibility or incompatibility between the two. An Internalizing Child is very susceptible to negative remarks or blatant manipulation. If you are a Strong-Willed Parent, you may easily become frustrated and even angry at what you perceive to be no forward movement in potty training. Recognize this now and take steps to control your own feelings because your child must do this at his or her own pace. If you are an Impulsive Parent, you might change tactics too quickly and not provide enough time for your Internalizing Daughter or Son to contemplate all the aspects of toileting. We urge you to breathe deeply and take it one step at a time.

Another dangerous trap for parents is misinterpreting slow progress as willful behavior on the part of their child. It's easy to jump to the conclusion that she/he is being disobedient or stubborn. This can set up a negative parent–child communication pattern, and it might also lead to a self-fulfilled prophecy (i.e., child is treated as Strong-Willed and therefore becomes somewhat Strong-Willed).

Remember, as we've mentioned throughout this book, parents can never force their child to go to the bathroom. Proper pacing is incredibly important. It's also a fine line you're going to have to walk; to balance on, really. Encourage without pressuring, go slow but keep moving forward, and ease fears without playing into them. Any way you look at it, potty training your child is likely to be a long journey, so plan for it. Pushing an Internalizer forward before they are ready will not potty train them more quickly; on the contrary, it will stall the process. If you try this, you'll find out just how close they are to becoming Strong-Willed! The idea behind all of our strategies is to allow your child to take the lead by subtly encouraging their interest.

Proper strategies will contribute to your Internalizer's self-confidence. He needs to know that he will be allowed to progress within his comfort zone. You're just going to have to go about potty training in a bit of a sideways manner—your main objective will be to enlarge his comfort zone to include the potty.

The Circle of Trust

Your child's comfort zone is her circle of trust. It's the physical and mental area in which she has the confidence of knowing the lay of the land. It's where she is familiar with the landmarks and knows the rules. It's where she can retreat from the myriad of anxieties that bombard her elsewhere; it's her oasis of calm. For most kids, the comfort zone is physically represented by their home, and understandably so. This is where they spend the most time and where they are surrounded by the people who love them most. This is where they feel safe.

Although the toilet is under the same roof (we hope!), it's not a part of your child's consciousness, so it isn't an official part of their comfort zone. Kids know that such contraptions, like the stove and washing machine, exist in the home, but they may not know what they are for and aren't yet comfortable around them. For the potty, anyway, this is about to change.

As discussed in the previous chapters, props can set the stage for potty training, and can expand the Internalizer's circle of trust. Storybooks can help you break through your Internalizing Daughter or Son's natural barriers. Stories allow children to observe and think about things without directly relating it to themselves. It's a safe, nonthreatening way for them to consider everything involved in going on the potty. Choose a book that has a main character your child can relate to—same gender and basic age. If your little Internalizer isn't your first child and you already have some story-books, don't worry about matching the gender as much because she/he will relate to the fact that this book once belonged to his or her sibling.

When you read the stories with your child, start by asking him to tell you what he thinks is going on. Have him look at the pictures and try to guess what the story will be about. Listen closely to what he tells you, as he may open up about any immediate worries. Read the story as written; there's no need to direct attention to the fact that this is something you want him to learn. We can guarantee that's already on his mind and, typically, he'll take the idea in and mull it over for a while. At the end of the book, you may be able to coax a conversation out of him by asking whether he has any questions about going potty, but don't push it. When he is ready, he'll come to you. If you can read stories in the bathroom, maybe before a bath or after you've role-modeled going potty, that may help bring the area of the toilet into their comfort zone.

While potty-training videos are a good thing to try, they are not necessary for most kids. However, they can be incredibly helpful with Internalizers. Remember, the more information you can give your child about going potty, the more comfortable she will feel about starting the process. Watching her favorite characters sing and dance about going potty will usually put her at ease. That said, all these props can get expensive, so don't buy them unless you can afford them. Videos are not an essential prop (if we had to advise you to choose spending money on a video or a book, the book would win every time), but a secondary activity to reinforce the lessons from the book. Check your local library for potty training books or videos; this will alleviate the expense while giving your child the benefits.

Dolls with potties can also be useful, for boys as well as girls. With other personality types, giving a doll to a boy who doesn't have any other dolls may come across as blatant manipulation, but an Internalizing Boy will more likely respond positively and enjoy the opportunity to role play with the doll. Girls may already have a collection of dolls and one more will fit right in. You don't need to present it as a doll for learning. Just give it as you would any other toy, explain what the potty is for if asked, and step back and let the child's imagination take over. Observe carefully though, and you may learn what your child thinks about pee, poop, or the potty. Again, purchasing a new doll for potty training is not something you have to do, but if the expense isn't an issue for you, it can give your child an additional means to bolster her or his self-confidence and expand that comfort zone.

A potty chair can also help your Internalizer ease into toilet training. It looks and feels similar to a toy, is at just the right height for a toddler or preschooler, and doesn't make any scary noises like the big potty. Introducing a potty chair will contribute much to alleviating your child's anxieties about the toilet, leaving more time for you to focus on building self-assurance in the bodily acts. If you're going to take your Internalizer along to shop for a potty chair, you should first do all of the preparatory work listed above to be sure that going on the potty is a skill he's already determined he wants to learn. If you don't, he may freeze up at the store when confronted by an array of potties. To avoid this problem, you might purchase (but save the receipts) three different chairs to bring home and allow your child to choose. When the foundation for potty training is laid and your child is ready to move forward, choosing his own potty chair can be an empowering first step. He will figuratively and literally own the process from here on out.

Place the potty chair wherever your child will be most comfortable trying it out. Locating it in the bathroom next to the big toilet would be best, if the bathroom has already become a part of your child's comfort zone. If it's not yet, it's perfectly fine to put it in the playroom, their bedroom, or anywhere that works for both of you. (If outside the bathroom, however, you may want to place a bathmat or something underneath to "catch" any spills.) From then on, allow your child to take the lead in determining whether he initially sits in his clothes or naked, and when he wants to seriously start the training.

If your child is particularly fearful of having an accident, you might want to take some extra time to talk about how accidents happen to everyone and then sensitively offer to show her. This can be a sort of amended Practice Session. For example, just before you put her in the tub for a bath you could demonstrate what pee-pee might feel like.

Potty Talk

Mom: Hey cutie, remember when we were talking earlier about going potty and you asked me about pee-pee accidents?

Child: Yes.

Mom: Well, I thought it might help you to see what it feels like . . . don't worry, you don't have to have a real accident. But when I turned on the water for your bath, I remembered that pee-pee sometimes feels like bath water. Here, I'll show you. (Take a small cup of the warm water and drizzle it over your own arm, not the child's.) See, it was just some warm water, but that's what pee-pee feels like if it comes out of you. Do you want to feel?

If your child says no, drop the subject for tonight, but try again another night. If she says yes, drizzle the water over her arm the same way you did it to yourself. If she is okay with that, offer to show her what it feels like on her legs because that's where it will be during a real accident. Then show her how you'll clean them up—you're going to give her a bath anyway!

In this way, again, you can give your child a safe simulation he can then mull over in his mind before the real thing ever happens. If you (and your child) want to take it to the next level, you could use some mud to simulate the feeling of poop on his legs. We know this is pretty weird advice, but these kinds of role-play activities may relieve your little Internalizer's anxiety enough to kick start the potty training, and, after all, that's what this book is all about!

One thing to keep in mind, especially for a parent of an Internalizer, is that there is a line between adapting appropriately to your child's anxieties and indulging them. It is easy for parents to become overly focused on making sure that all of their child's anxieties are addressed to the point that these kinds of traits are inadvertently reinforced in the child.

It is a little of the self-fulfilling prophecy—if you treat them like fragile children, they become more fragile. It's a tough balancing act. For the purposes of potty training, it may be better to err on the side of indulging them a little. If you run into serious anxiety and resistance, the best option is to simply take a small break from potty training.

First Steps

There is a very blurry line between the end of the preparatory steps and the beginning of the actual training steps in potty training the Internalizing Child. Because your daughter or son will silently contemplate the subject matter internally for a long time, she/he will take incremental moves forward. You may not even be aware of the progress at first.

For the purposes of this chapter, the actual toilet training begins when your child starts to sit on the pot naked; in other words, when the possibility exists of a successful first pee or poop. From this point on, you can urge them on in more dynamic ways. Keep the expectations and pressure off, but you can now be more obvious in your prodding through the use of Practice Sessions.

Invite your child to sit on her potty when you are sitting on yours. Hand her some toilet paper so she can pretend to wipe herself. Let her wash her hands while you wash yours. Teach her the meaning behind the old adage, "practice makes perfect," but keep the emphasis on the practicing instead of the perfection.

Potty Dialog

Increase your potty dialog to include more about how you recognize the urge to go, how you try before you leave the house, and how you rush to the bathroom when you need to. Use as many examples as you can. Offer hypothetical situations and discuss how you and your child might react. Allow him or her to thoroughly consider different likely scenarios.

Potty Talk

Dad: You're doing a great job sitting on the potty and trying to go, but what if you were outside on the playground when you felt like the pee-pee needed to come out? What would you do?

Child: I'd run to the bathroom!

Dad: (respond positively to any answer that's close to right): Great! And what would you do if you had to go in the middle of watching *Sesame Street*?

Child: Ummm . . .

Dad: (lightheartedly): You'd run to the bathroom then, too, right?

Child: Right!

Dad: Because you could go real fast and then come back to finish watching *Sesame Street*, right? You wouldn't miss a thing. You're really getting the hang of this potty stuff!

You shouldn't go overboard, but occasionally throw out a made-up circumstance and ask your child how he or she would react. These kinds of question and answer sessions will serve two purposes; first, it will give your kid the chance to contemplate different possibilities, and second, it will be a way to prompt him or her to think about going potty a number of times throughout the day.

Scheduling

At this juncture, your child will need a lot of prompting. Internalizers will likely be very receptive to the idea of sitting and trying at periodic times throughout the day. Their tendency to careful forethought is going to work right into potty training now, because they'll know what might happen if they don't try to go and they will want to avoid having an accident. Unlike Impulsive Children who won't remember or really care about the danger of an accident, and unlike Strong-Willed Children who don't want anyone else telling them what to do, your Internalizing Son or Daughter will probably relish the Hop on the Pot idea of sitting at regularly scheduled times and trying to go. She/he probably won't get too discouraged if nothing happens at first, but will be elated at the first success.

If your child does go, then it gives you the opportunity to express your amazement. Be sure not to communicate it in the tone of, "Now you've done it once, I expect the same every time." Instead, the message you send should be one of happy surprise. The idea is for you to give your child every opportunity to perform without any overtly communicated expectation to perform.

> *Mom: Wow, I sure didn't expect you to go pee-pee, but you did it! That's exactly what is supposed to happen—but with a lot of kids it takes a lot longer to go pee on the potty—I'm really impressed! I sure did not think that would happen this time. Great job!*

As with the other categories of children, the Internalizer's usual elimination schedule should be monitored before potty training is begun. Plan Practice Sessions for when your child is most likely to pee, and perhaps offer an extra cup or two of water ten to fifteen minutes before a planned try. Practicing on the potty or toilet at regular intervals throughout the day is a fantastic tactic with an Internalizing Kid. You could even set the kitchen timer for every half hour, and make a game of it.

Training Diapers

Normally, we aren't big fans of training diapers that you just pull on and off. They don't absorb enough to prevent messes but do absorb enough to provide an excuse to not use the potty. However, we recognize that, particularly with Internalizing Children, an accident can be traumatizing. Training diapers are a small, very small, step forward in the process, but they may be a giant leap in your child's mind and we respect that. If she/he has especially acute fears about accidents, or if you've already made an aborted attempt at potty training and anxiety is running high, pull-ons can be a very useful tool. The key to avoiding all of this is taking potty training very slow and easy, and if these help you do that then more power to you! We'd urge you to be vigilant though. Continue everything else you're doing while the child is wearing the training diaper and resist the urge, for either you or your child, to become dependent on them. So, instead of going from diapers to underpants, you present pull-ons as a transitional item around the same time your child sits on the potty naked for the first time.

Potty Practice

Practice sessions on the potty or toilet should continue as often as possible. If you're a stay-at-home parent, this won't be too difficult except for the need to forego outings for a little while. If you work and your child is cared for by someone else, they may or may not be able to continue with your exact schedule. Make the request and see what kind of response you get. However, large daycare centers probably won't be able to do a potty break every half hour. Explain this in simple terms to your child and coach him to request a potty break whenever he feels like he needs one. Have a sit-down meeting with the childcare provider to discuss ways to make potty training as similar as possible to what you're doing at home. Involve your child in this, because he should be an active participant in the plan. Perhaps you could get a watch with an alarm that he could wear; you could teach him that when the alarm goes off he should take a potty break. That way, the teacher isn't beholden to remember every half hour, and your child is provided another means to "own" the process.

Nakedtime

Nakedtime is a practice we've touted a great deal in this book, and it has its benefits with any kind of temperament. We suggest you read back through the nakedtime sections of Chapter 3. Nearly every child, given the opportunity, will relish the idea of running around naked. Internalizers, however, may be more reticent than others. They may react similarly to the Sensory-Oriented Child, so you should take precautions for comfort, safety, and quick clean-ups. If you are going to do nakedtime outside, make sure the temperature isn't too warm or too chilly. In addition, kids who internalize will be mindful of whether any outsiders can observe them, so be respectful of their feelings. Their natural wariness is an asset, so don't discourage or try to break them of the habit. We mentioned it earlier, but if you have a swing set you'll have to determine which activities are safe to play on while naked. Again, like the Sensory-Oriented Kids, Internalizers may react badly to the mess, so have all your cleaning supplies within easy reach. If you're conducting nakedtime inside your house, determine which rooms are off-limits and plan plenty of activities for the "wait."

Internalizers, though, will require more information and forewarning than Sensory-Oriented Children about what will happen while they are naked. Being up front and honest about what kind of game this is will allow them to wrap their mind around the idea first. You could give them a few hours or even a day to think about it. Explain the possibility of an accident in matter-of-fact terms, without making it sound scary, and then give assurances that you'll be right there to help them get to the potty or get cleaned up.

The major benefit to nakedtime is that your child can see what his or her body produces and connect it immediately to the associated feelings. With an Internalizer, you may want to take an almost clinical approach when describing everything. Share with your child how his or her body works, in an age-appropriate manner, of course, and make it clear this is a natural process that happens with everyone. By depersonalizing it, your child may be better able to understand that eliminating the body's waste is not something to be overly concerned about. Again, it's all about widening that individual comfort zone to include these practices.

Accidents

What do you do if, despite everyone's best efforts, your Internalizer's first experience isn't a success but an accident? As empowering as the first pee-pee experience can be, if it doesn't happen into the potty, it can be just as powerful in a negative way. To a child who, even at this young age, wants everything to be perfect, an accident can be truly traumatizing.

Accidents manifest themselves differently depending on a kid's personality type. Whereas a Strong-Willed Child, for example, will get angry, an Internalizer will become demoralized, quickly retreat into herself, and attempt to abandon the effort. Your job is to manage the crisis of an accident so that your child maintains any recently found confidence, acknowledge that accidents will happen, and teach her that it isn't the end of the world—all this in a calm manner while you clean her up as quickly as possible. Talk about multitasking!

This is where you fall back on all the preliminary steps you took with your child before toilet training began in earnest. In every child's storybook, there should be mention of having accidents. Hopefully, you've talked with him early and often about the fact that everyone has accidents when they're learning how to go pee-pee and poop in the toilet. If you tried the warm water and mud simulation in the bathtub, your child may even have felt the physical sensation of having an accident. But this is the first time he's feeling the emotional sensations of a failure, and it will be a big blow to his pride no matter how well you've prepared him. It is natural for almost anyone to get a little defensive if they mess up, and so a little defensiveness should not be overinterpreted as anything more than a natural and temporary reaction. Most often with Internalizers, the accidents are not a direct conduit to a power struggle, but be on the lookout for Strong-Willed tendencies to surface.

When the first accident happens, respond quickly and calmly. If she is really upset—crying, shaking, and scared—talk her through it with an even voice; get close to her ear so she can hear you through her panic. Take her into a private room if you are not alone. If it's a milder reaction, comfort her as you see fit without making too much of the accident. Simply reiterate that these things happen to everyone, that you'll clean her right up, and maybe change the focus onto yourself by talking about a time when it happened to you as a child. Make up a story, if you have to, about an accident you had when you were first learning to go on the potty. In your child's eyes, you are the Golden Standard for everything, so relating a time when you failed at something just like she did will relieve a bit of the pressure she's put on herself to accomplish this potty-training goal perfectly.

Mom: Oh, sweetie, you had an accident. It's okay—it happens to everyone. Let's go get you changed into some clean clothes. You know, this exact same thing happened to me when I was a little girl. Yup, I was trying to learn how to go pee-pee on the potty, and I had some accidents, too. At first it scared me a little and I was worried I might not ever learn how to do it right, but Grandma helped me and pretty soon I got the hang of it.

After a few more accidents, if your child is feeling discouraged and worried that he may never learn, you could add something like, "I had a whole lot more accidents than you have, though. I think I must have had about a million accidents!" And then laugh a little at yourself and change the subject. This will boost your child's self-esteem, because, of course, he hasn't had a million accidents, so he's doing better than you.

There is a delicate balance between sensitive acknowledgment and indulgence of the behavior, however. In other words, don't inadvertently condone or give too much permission for the unwanted behavior—recognize it and move on to a form of positive reinforcement that will assist your child to continue on track. If your child seems to be stuck wallowing in self-pity over a string of accidents, try addressing it head on. Yours is the type of kid who is a rational thinker, so use that to your advantage.

Dad: I can see having another accident has really upset you. I can understand how it makes you feel bad. Let's get you cleaned right up and next time we will make sure you have shorts on that are easier to pull down.

The trap that many Internalizers fall into is that if they feel they are having an inordinate amount of accidents—and to a child this number could be illogically low—their insecurities become magnified. The anxiety will cause their body to tense when it comes time to go, which in turn will mean they have trouble eliminating. Then it cycles back through again: not being able to go equals lack of potty success and that makes them tense up even more next time. They get it in their head that they cannot be successful, so future attempts at potty training are met with instant anxiety (like a form of performance anxiety). In addition, tenseness can lead children to become "holders," that is, withholding their stools. This makes it uncomfortable to go when they do go. Discomfort equals more holding, which causes more discomfort and then more holding. If let go too long, constipation can develop. Sometimes, to stop this vicious cycle, you may have to backtrack to a point in the process where they can be successful and then start again to build up their self-confidence.

The Dirty Diaper

Sylvia and Louis noticed their son, Ricky, had constipation* issues. He would go three, four, sometimes even five days before he finally pooped. When he did finally go, it would be a long episode of sitting on the toilet (or, at first, hiding somewhere with his training diaper on) and crying in anticipation. "Pooping for him was a psychological hurdle," said his mom, who realized only time would cure the situation. After a while, Louis decided to link pooping to one of Ricky's favorite games, basketball. He talked with his son about sinking a basket and how all the greatest players have to practice a lot before they get good at it. He also made the gentle point that hard work gets easier the more often you do it. Slowly, very slowly, Ricky started getting better about pooping. When something is bothering him, the constipation does come back, but now Ricky can work through it a little easier.

Some relaxation techniques can be incredibly helpful in these types of situations. Make the bathroom a comfortable place for your Internalizer. Similar to the Sensory-Oriented Child in Chapter 5, ask for input on the kind of soap, towels, or toilet paper so that she will feel at home in the bathroom. Make sure she can reach everything she needs; keep a step stool by the potty and sink. Store some favorite books in there, too, or even some paper and crayons. If your child has some favorite soothing

*You can read more about constipation problems in Chapter 10.

music, bring the CD player into the bathroom and turn it on! (Of course, keep power cords away from the water areas to prevent electric shock.) All of this sets a relaxing mood for success.

Nighttime Dryness

Nighttime dryness will likely take a while to achieve, and Internalizers are no different from any others in this regard. To ensure the process stays stress free, keep your toddler or preschooler in diapers at night until you start to notice his diaper is dry when he wakes up. At this point, you will know his muscles are strong enough to regulate output even during the subconscious state. This does not mean he will not have accidents. Even children who have been trained for years still occasionally have accidents at night. Follow the tactics outlined in Chapter 3, Universal Strategies, about alleviating nighttime accidents by limiting liquid intake, and ways you can do a quick clean up.

Most children will be upset by an accident in the middle of the night, particularly if they wake up far after the fact and they are soaking wet and cold. Parents should continue with the same matter-of-fact, relaxed reassurances. You may be able to simply clean her up, change the sheets, and get her back to sleep with as little disruption as possible. If she's really upset, speak calmingly into her ear and deal with those feelings first. Save the potty-training discussion until morning, unless your child is fully awake and wants to talk about it. If this is the case, work to normalize it as much as possible. Tell her a story (make it up if you have to) about how the same thing happened to you when you were learning how to stay dry at night. Everyone has accidents; that's how we learn.

There are some Internalizers who may become superfocused on continued nighttime accidents. It's possible he may view this as a failure, despite whatever success you've had during the day. Be sure to communicate that there is no shame in having an accident. Again, use logic to your advantage and explain that unlike daytime dryness, when your child is awake to command his muscles, nighttime dryness is much less controllable.

If you think it would not make him feel worse, you could ask if he would like to go back to wearing diapers for a little while. Explain that a good night's rest is essential to his overall health and that you can try for nighttime dryness again soon. You don't want to abandon this effort, but if accidents are occurring every night despite all attempts to stop them, it could just be that his body is not ready to take control yet.

Some children, of any temperament, cannot reliably stay dry at night until age 5, at which point you may want to consider talking it over with your pediatrician to determine if there are any other factors contributing to the problem.

Follow-Through

A good follow-through tactic with the Internalizer is to separate pee-pee training from training to poop in the potty. These kids benefit greatly from breaking down the process, not only in potty training but in anything they need to learn. Tackling five small tasks is not as daunting as one, large, overarching goal. Again, we suggest reading back through Chapter 3 for additional information, as the tactics are basically the same for the Internalizer.

The pacing of lessons is key here. It is going to be a long haul with your Internalizing Son or Daughter, so plan for it. Pushing your child forward before she or he is ready will not bring success more quickly; it will have the opposite effect and shrink the circle of trust.

When learning the higher-order skills of toileting, these kids will have to go through the same thinking process they did with each step before, so be sure to give them plenty of information and time to consider their preferred first move. Back off for a little while in between the major skills. At some point in their development, you're likely to see them take something on their own initiative, and this is when you're home free. An Internalizer, after he's worked through his potty-training anxiety issues, will often transform into a Goal-Directed Child. If you're lucky, this may occur closer to the beginning of the process, but, alas, with most kids, it happens toward the end. Continue to impart as much information as you can, answering his questions in a forthright manner, and providing positive feedback on his advancement.

•••

Internalizers prefer to think through everything before they act. Because potty training is their first independent milestone, this may be the first time you really see their preference take over. Offering toileting information to your child early and often will go a long way, as will taking some presteps outlined at the beginning of this chapter.

From there, inserting the bathroom and other toileting activities into your child's comfort zone, or circle of trust, will similarly help. Take care in using praise to reinforce his sense of success and mitigate any accidents. Again, parents of Internalizers need to plan for the long haul and not push a child too fast. Make sure you communicate these personality traits to your child's caregivers, whether that be a daycare center, nanny or grandparents, so that everyone helping your child potty train is doing so in a consistent manner that takes his preferences into account. In these ways, your child will be successful, and will feel empowered by the experience of learning these important skills.

7

The Impulsive Child

mpulsive Children are relatively easy to spot. They are the ones who are into everything, jump from one ambitious activity to another, find ways to turn anything into a toy or a game, and never seem to tire. You may just as easily spot the parents of an Impulsive Child—they're usually sweaty from nonstop running, unable to hold a conversation with another adult for too long because they can't take their eyes off their kid, and their homes are baby-proofed to the hilt.

In this chapter, parents will learn how to focus an Impulsive Child on the task of potty training, hold her interest, and work on needed skills within her attention span. The Universal Strategy of Role Modeling is key, as is reinforcing the type of behavior you want to see your child repeat. Finally, we'll go through one of the toughest skills an Impulsive Child will need to learn, which is patience, particularly in terms of trying to go often and waiting for nature to take its course.

The Impulsive Temperament

Impulsive children are energetic and active. They constantly seek out new ways to stimulate themselves, which is why they are frequently described as easily distractible. They seldom or never sit still. Part of this is attributable to a certain dexterity—often early walkers, these kids are agile, nimble, and always looking for the next fun, exciting activity. They master physical skills quickly, don't like to be bored, and relentlessly challenge themselves. Bodily risk-takers, they're the ones who climb all over the furniture. These are the kids for whom safety latches were invented.

They always want to do things bigger and better than before. Impulsive Children place great importance on, and take great pride in, being the fastest and the first. Naturally, they tend to get caught up in activities. They also enjoy rough-and-tumble play, and frequently are the children who take this too far and, without intending to, end up hurting a playmate.

They are easily excitable and anticipate everything as a great adventure. They may have quick negative reactions that lead into tantrum behavior. But being typically happy children, they recover quickly from being upset and are usually adaptable. They easily interact with familiar and unfamiliar people or situations. For the Impulsive Child, every day is a new day and she/he lives for the moment.

Think Curious George® and you've got the picture.

Potty training is not the kind of activity that will usually hold the interest of an Impulsive Child for very long. By design, there's a great deal of sitting and waiting involved, two things these kids don't like to do. In the beginning, of course, using the potty is the new, exciting thing and you probably won't have trouble getting your Impulsive Child interested in the process. She will love the idea of going in the potty, just like Mommy and Daddy. Like other physical activities, she may get the hang of that part of it fairly quickly. However, after just a few successes she may become bored, feel she's already mastered this skill, and look to move onto something more challenging. You will struggle to get her to sit still long enough to stimulate her bladder, not to mention her colon!

Your Impulsive Son or Daughter won't have much interest in focusing on his or her bodily functions enough to get too far into potty training. Impulsive Children also have a hard time stopping a favored activity to do something they may soon consider a chore. In their minds, diapers are just easier, and therefore preferred.

In potty training, there is a difference between recognizing the signs and noticing the signs. It's an extremely fine line, but recognition is intellectually learning to associate the signs of needing to go with the actual act, whereas noticing is real-time awareness of the signs when they occur. Impulsive Children in particular will have a hard time noticing the signs of impending elimination. Even when they're doing the "dance," they will not connect the feeling with the need to go. They simply aren't focused on those feelings or muscles. Whatever it is they are focused on at that time—a game, a friend, a meal—will cloud over anything else. The difficulty for you will be breaking through that cloud cover. Even when you do get through to them, and they learn to associate the feeling with the function, they may continue to have trouble noticing the feeling when it does occur. They are simply paying more attention to other things.

The keys to potty training Impulsive Children are scheduling, prompting, and directing their focus. With these children more so than others, you'll have to build in some pit-stops throughout the day. Keeping their interest alive will also be a test.

First Steps

Regular Routine

Subtle changes in your family's routine, even before beginning an intense focus on potty training, can make a difference with an Impulsive Child. Most children, regardless of their personality type, learn best by observing and imitating the adults who are most influential in their life. Plan to act out the behavior your child will have the most trouble with—noticing the urge to go and stopping another activity to do so.

Start by giving yourself a potty break before you leave the house or begin a big project. Call attention to it so your child sees that you are making an effort to try to go to the bathroom at specific times. Explain that you, too, dislike having to stop doing something fun to take a potty break. Perhaps even talk about a time you didn't stop and had an accident. Bring her or him into the bathroom with you. An Impulsive Child usually understands the physical mechanics of going to the bathroom before the emotional aspects of when and why.

Role Modeling

Modeling behavior is very important for the Impulsive Child. Show her how you make time for bathroom breaks and then go do more fun stuff. Talk with her about how you feel when you really have to go.

Mom: Oh boy, my tummy is starting to hurt a little and it feels really full. I feel like pee-pee might need to come out. We'd better take a break and so I can go to the potty. I'll be right back and then we can finish playing our game.

Some of it may be embarrassing, and yes, your child might repeat it to a perfect stranger or your boss, but that just means she is taking it to heart.

Although modeling behavior like this is an important part of toilet training, this alone will not train your son or daughter.

The way a parent approaches this can make or break the strategy. You are narrating the action to get her to notice what you are doing, and eventually to copy it, but this is simply the first act in a multistep process. Keep the modeling behavior about you and you alone—for now—but know that with every conversation, you are building the foundation on which the rest of potty training will be based.

> *Dad: Gosh, we are about to go to the store and I don't know if there will be a potty there. But you know what? I kind of have the feeling that I have to use the potty. So, I think that I will go before we leave. Why don't you come with me as I do that?*

In this approach, the parent communicates everything they should, but in a way that focuses only on the parent. This is a very nonthreatening method to communicate the point.

The first line of resistance that most kids (Impulsive or otherwise) will give when asked to try before leaving the house is that they don't need to go. For all kids, especially the Impulsive Ones, parents need to place a lot of emphasis on the trying behavior in the beginning. You can role model this as well. Here's an amended version of the above dialog:

> *Dad: Gosh, we are about to go to the store and I don't know if there will be a potty there. I don't really feel like I have to go, but I think I'll just try real fast just in case. (Then, when nothing happens) Hmmm . . . maybe there just isn't any pee-pee that needs to come out right now. Oh well, I gave it a try, and now we can go to the store.*

The message you are directing to the child is that activities are interrupted to try to go to the bathroom, regardless of whether the need is felt. This eliminates the potential argument with the child later on and you can say, "I did not ask whether you feel like you have to go—I asked you to go the bathroom and try." Trying is really the behavior that should be of most interest to parents at this stage. Also, down the road, well after the child is potty trained, parents will likely find that they need to continue to remind their Impulsive Kids to try. Therefore, the stage for a "trying" routine should be set, and practiced before starting an activity or heading out of the house for the day. Here is another example dialog:

> *Mom: Are you ready to go swing on the swings? Okay, let's go! Oh, wait just a second . . . we better try to go pee-pee because there's no potty at the park. Come on, let's do that real quick before we go and then we won't have to come home early just to go to the bathroom!*

Later on, when he is faced with the same kinds of decisions, he'll know this is the right approach to going potty. You will also have the opportunity to remind him that everyone has to make time to go to the bathroom, even when they don't want to. As discussed previously, parents have control only over their own behavior, and can only manage the process with their children. Thoughtful, strategic management practices are in order and much of this will revolve around giving good directions, praise, positive encouragement, and effective communication. In this way, you can assist your child to be successful, but you cannot do it for them. Your Impulsive Child will still need to work through this at his or her natural pace.

Once your daughter or son does become interested, she or he will probably want to get on the toilet immediately. If you're lucky, it'll be at a time when she or he does have to go and you'll have an early accomplishment to build on! More often than not, nothing will come out but your child's curiosity will be piqued. From then on, you can include her or him in the family's routine. We suggest approaching this as potty practice time that is treated no differently than other customary daily tasks, such as brushing teeth, bathing, and picking up toys. It's just one of those things everyone does. Setting this up as a customary routine ensures that they expect to be asked to try to go pee-pee before leaving the house. Be sure to use the strategy of Giving Good Directions, and be extra specific with your Impulsive Child. If the habit is set and observed by them long before the potty-training process begins, it can diminish the kinds of daily power struggles that many families of Impulsive Children face.

Again, having a schedule for your child to sit on the potty will not alone train him, but it is one important way for you to influence the process, effectively set the stage, and hopefully have some timely success.

Reinforcing Behavior

Rewards may work with Impulsive Children, for a time. But they will quickly learn how to up the ante, and will request bigger, better rewards until you're restocking the playroom after each bathroom break! If you choose this method, you'll need to start small and keep it tightly under control, unless you have room for a pony in the backyard.

Parents should use praise and positive statements as the best kind of reward. No child ever gets tired of this, and it is always appropriate. In time, kids will be motivated by their own sense of accomplishment and their parents' positive regard. As with children of each personality type, Impulsive Children should be praised most for behaviors at which they have to work the hardest. This kind of dialog will be incredibly empowering:

Dad: I'm so proud of my princess for remembering to go potty all day today! You've been working so hard to go as soon as you feel like you have to, and you're doing great! Let's see if we can do something special tomorrow to celebrate all your hard work.

You can capitalize on the Impulsive Child's inherent competitive attitude to get them to focus. Without putting them into direct competition with the other kids in their play group or daycare class, you can point out random children at the mall or any public place and mention the kinds of things they get to do because they've learned to go in the toilet.

Mom: Do you see that girl up there? I can tell she's wearing big-girl underwear, and I'll bet that's why she can spend a longer time than us here at the science center. Being able to go pee-pee and poop on the potty means she gets to do more fun things like this.

Before you begin the actual training, you could even manufacture a bit of a disappointment for your child, by pretending to run out of diapers and having to cut an outing short. (If you're like us, it'll probably happen to you in the course of everyday life and you won't have to pretend!) Take care not to do this during the early days of training, or you'll sabotage the entire process. And, don't choose a much-anticipated event to cut short—that's not fair—instead, a regular trip to the park or store will serve the same purpose. A letdown like this is something they'll remember, giving you fodder for a reminder later on.

Dad: Remember that time we had to leave because we had to go home and get a new diaper? I'm so proud of all the hard work you've been doing to stay dry in your big-boy underwear. Now, we can stay in fun places longer. You're doing so great!

This kind of positive reinforcement, tied directly to the effort that they are putting into going potty, is very fitting.

Potty Chairs

For some Impulsive Kids, using the toilet will be important to them; they will really get into it and be relatively easy to train. Some will give off such obvious signals that a parent will be able to prompt them and get them to the potty in time. However, Impulsive Children are characteristically unpredictable and do not want to stop a more exciting activity to go into the bathroom. Potty chairs are popular with kids because of their small, cutesy look, but their portability is the significant selling point for parents of Impulsive Children.

As with any other potty-training method, having a general idea of your child's elimination schedule and increasing reminders when it gets close to the usual time will be helpful. Because children of this temperament have a tough time noticing the urge to pee or poop, having a potty you can take from room to room in your house, or even in the car or at the park, will be helpful. To put it another way, transit time is of the essence.

The Dirty Diaper

To give you a vivid snapshot of the dangers, we'll share with you the story of Melissa, the mom of a three-year-old Impulsive Girl named Meaghan. Melissa, who is Impulsive herself, kept getting distracted from the potty-training process. She sometimes neglected to carry the potty chair along as Meaghan moved from room to room. Plus, Meaghan didn't really give off predictable signs she had to go, and so they'd had a few peeing accidents. But nothing too out of the ordinary happened until the afternoon of Meaghan's third day in underwear. Melissa took a phone call from work and got a little caught up in the conversation. After a few minutes, she looked back to check on Meaghan, only to be horrified to see her looking around in vain for the potty, and, when she didn't find it, squatting to poop on the brand new carpet. Melissa, who was just hanging up the phone, stretched out with her free hand and dove under Meaghan. She caught the poop and managed not to gag as she rushed Meaghan and herself to the bathroom to get cleaned up. It wasn't until the next day at work when her boss, chuckling, told her the line hadn't cut off and she'd heard the whole incident! Luckily, she'd been through a tough potty-training phase with her own kids and was duly impressed with Melissa's quick "save."

You'll need to follow your Impulsive Son or Daughter along fairly closely with the potty chair. When your child moves from one activity to another, you should unfailingly pick up the potty and bring it with you. You don't need to make a big deal about it, but make sure he knows where it is when he needs it. Having one at hand for immediate use will increase the likelihood of success from the beginning. Your child learns to pee and poop right there. You stop buying diapers, put your child in underwear, and hurrah! You're not done with the process, but congratulations are certainly in order anyway.

After a good amount of success this way, start "accidentally" leaving the potty in another room or maybe in the bathroom after cleaning it. When your child has to go, she now has to hold her pee/poop until she can get to the room with the potty chair or to the bathroom. It may be just 20 extra steps, but you're training her how to use her muscles to hold it. Each week, make the potty a little more scarce. Soon, she'll get the hang of controlling her muscles and will head for the bathroom before the pee-pee or poop comes out. If you alternate with times when she has to run to the toilet instead of the potty chair, you will have an easier transition to the actual toilet. But, again, like many of our methods, you can alter the steps of the training process to suit your particular child.

Parents of Impulsive Children run a greater risk than many others of being one step behind. Sometimes the impulsiveness is inherited, as with many other traits. If your child is just too active and you have a hard time following along with the potty (or remembering to bring it with you from room to room), or if you can't get a handle on the schedule or signals, you may want to consider getting several potties to scatter around your house. We know of one mom who bought a potty for every room in her home! Of course this can get expensive and you won't win an award for interior design, but it can get your child out of diapers. Parents of Impulsive Children must always be proactive planners—paying lots of attention to patterns and signs. Sometimes more extreme measures are warranted.

It may be embarrassing, or even feel indecent to bring a potty chair to a friend's house or sit your child down on it in the middle of the park, but you won't be the first parent to do this and your concern should be choosing the method that will work best for your child. Impulsive Children usually do not mind an audience when they go, but certainly find out first. If your child, or you, feels uncomfortable bringing the potty out in public, keep it on the floor of the car and take care to stay nearby. Bringing a potty along is necessary, because if you want to cement your training, you cannot put your Impulsive Children back into diapers for outings or they'll unlearn what they have been taught. Having an accident because there isn't a potty nearby can erode your child's sense of accomplishment and is emotionally defeating.

Many a parent of an Impulsive Child (your illustrious author, Sara, included) has trained their child by carting one of these lovely items around—everywhere—for months. From the back yard to the kitchen, the living room to the minivan, Sara took her son's little blue potty wherever they went. At times (specifically at the community playground), she felt ridiculous. But you know what? Making it that much of an integral part of their lives was a nonverbal way to punctuate the importance of giving her son whatever support he needed to learn these skills. And, it worked. His self-confidence grew and with that came greater muscular control, as well as an understanding of the feelings that signal the need to go to the bathroom. What hasn't yet come to this Impulsive Boy is the value of trying to go pee even when he doesn't need to go—they're still working on that one! Sara even admits to having a pang of nostalgia when they were finished with the little blue potty because it was such an important part of crossing this milestone with her firstborn.

------- **Training Tip** -----------------

> Take quick cleanup materials, including plastic bags, extra wipes, tissues, and hand sanitizer with you wherever you take the potty.

As your child learns the signs of needing to go and the value of trying before leaving home, in addition to training his or her body to hold it for a little while, you should be able to start leaving the potty behind. It may take a while for Impulsive Kids to really get all this, though. Many parents like the convenience and keep a potty on hand in the car for emergencies. There is a fold-up kind that you can get at most baby stores that is compact and easy to use.

Nakedtime

Parents of Impulsive Children, like those of Goal-Directed Children, should be able to layer different strategies together to potty train. A natural combination is the use of the potty chair with sessions of nakedtime, described in Chapter 3. Nakedtime is a very beneficial tactic with Impulsive Kids because it makes the process of elimination tangible. They can see with their own eyes that "stuff" doesn't just magically appear in the diaper—it actually comes out of them.

Nakedtime is passive and requires no extra effort on the part of the parent or child until the first accident occurs. It's a fun, new, exciting thing and sure to capture your Impulsive Child's interest enough to make it through a few accidents, during which time you can teach some potty-training lessons and get the process going.

Choose your nakedtime area carefully, with the understanding that, because your child tends to be very physically active, the opportunity for a big mess is increased. The safety measures, suggested in Chapter 3, should be of particular concern, and you may want to create plenty of other activities to have on hand in between the main events.

Waiting for the Poop

Let's face it; pooping usually takes a lot longer than peeing. Most people have to wait for it, at least for a few minutes. Impulsive Children, in particular, have a hard time sitting still and waiting. Keeping some books in the bathroom may be helpful, or if your Impulsive Child hasn't been bitten by the book bug yet (many don't like sitting still for stories either!), singing songs and making up silly games while waiting for the poop can work, too. If you get really desperate, bring in a lap desk for her to use for coloring with paper and crayons.

Directing your child to a potty chair at times when he is more likely to have to poop—in the playroom, next to the kitchen table, or really anywhere—may also help minimize unproductive time on the potty. Again, having something like a book on hand to occupy him as he sits will help.

If you just cannot get your child to stay on the potty long enough to poop, as a last resort, try placing the potty chair in front of the television so he will sit for a longer period of time. To be clear, we are not advocating excessive television viewing, but we are realists and parents ourselves. Most children are allowed to watch some television at this age, and combining the times during which your usually active kid has an incentive to sit still with learning to potty train, which requires stillness, may be a good short-term tactic. A concern, however, is that kids will become so focused on the show that they won't notice when they have peed or pooped. If you do feel like you have to use the television to get your child to sit still long enough, you should monitor them closely for signs of "action" and bring it to their attention. Otherwise, it'll be a useless lesson because he will not have learned the mechanics of going on the potty. Once he has had one or two successes, make a quick transition from the potty chair to the actual toilet. After all, you don't want your child to have a permanent association between the television and going potty. As stated in Chapter 3, Impulsive Kids are notorious for getting sucked into video games and television because few things compete with the level of convenient stimulation that these provide. And, please, choose an educational TV program!

Reminders, Reminders, Reminders

With Impulsive Children, in particular, you'll need to keep an eagle eye for signs that they have to go potty, and point them out. It may take a while for you to identify what your child's particular signs are. He or she may deny that they need to go, so let them have an accident or two, and then after they are cleaned up, talk to them about recognizing the signs you've identified. Parents should also be prepared to continuously hear, "I don't have to go," from their Impulsive Sons and Daughters. So, instead of asking, "Do you need to use the potty?" say something like, "You look like you need to use the potty—let's go!"

If the child truly does not have to go, then you can simply say it was a practice drill and move along. You'll have to continuously remind Impulsive Children for what may seem like forever, but because they are fairly adaptable, they will eventually realize that it's easier to simply get up and go to the bathroom than to have an accident that takes them away from their favored activity for longer.

"Do you have to go before we leave?" is a question that Parents of Impulsive Children will repeat millions of times over several years. It can become so ingrained into the brain that some parents continue to say it to their adult children! Again, instead of posing a question, to which your Impulsive Child will nearly always answer, "No," make it a routine for everyone in the family. Start this habit for the rest of the family before you potty train your child so that she/he will take it for granted. There is a fine line between harping and reminding. Try to stay on the reminding side, so you don't turn your child off to the idea of trying before going out. Remaining matter of fact will set the right tone for your child.

Potty Talk

Mom: We're going out so everyone needs to try to go to the bathroom.

Child: But I don't have to go!

Mom: Well, everyone has to try. If you don't have any pee-pee that comes out, it's okay, you just have to try to go. I just did and Daddy's trying now. Next it's your turn.

It's important for parents to remember that they are only the facilitators in the potty-training process. Parents can only coach kids to try to go, but they can't make them go. You'll need to have rules, based on your own family, about what constitutes "trying." Our suggestion is that children go into the bathroom, pull down their pants, and sit on the potty for thirty seconds. If it helps, keep a kitchen timer in the bathroom.

Parents should, however, be ready to forgive the times when their child appropriately tries to go before leaving the house, then ten minutes later has an accident. Sometimes it really does come on that quickly for Impulsive Kids, even just a few minutes after they made a good-faith effort. This should not be treated as a major infraction or blatant oppositional behavior. Keep a calm, straightforward demeanor. Acknowledge the accident without making a big deal about it. Clean the child as quickly as you can, explaining that this happens to everyone sometimes and it's the reason you all try to go before leaving home. Carry an extra set of clothes in the car. Provide any positive feedback about how they are handling the accident, and assure them that they'll soon be able to stay dry in underwear.

Dad: I know you're sad you had an accident, but I'm really proud of how you're helping me clean up now. You tried before we left home, but I guess the pee-pee wasn't ready to come out then. It came out here when we didn't have a potty nearby. That happens to everyone sometimes, but I know you're trying really hard and pretty soon you'll get the hang of it!

At some point, however, it's important to move beyond the "accidents are no big deal" stage. It's natural for kids to lose a little interest after the initial success. Remember that Impulsive Kids are always looking for the next new, exciting thing to master. Once they believe they know how to go potty, even if they don't yet have all the necessary skills, they may simply lose their incentive to continue the process. So, you'll need to find incentives for them. The necessity to stop an activity because of an accident can send a strong message to your Impulsive Child. For example, if you have to leave the park because of an accident, your child will be motivated to do it better next time. The natural consequence sends the message, not the parent.

Mom: We need to go home to get you cleaned up and changed. Gosh, that's too bad; we were having so much fun here. I guess we'll just have to come back another time.

Then, the thoughtful parent will tuck this experience away to use in the future when their Impulsive Toddler or Preschooler resists going potty.

Mom: Hey, do you remember that time we were at the park and you had an accident and we had to go home? If you have an accident, we'll have to go home again, so why don't you try to use the potty before we go, so we can stay there longer and have fun?

The point in this scenario needs to be communicated in a thoughtful manner. Take care not to use guilt-inducing words in frustration. Your tone should convey that you are on your child's side and that you want to stay at the activity and have fun just as much as she does. You are her partner for success, and each step forward gets you closer to the goal. The path forward may be zigzagged instead of straight with Impulsive Kids, but if you know this going in, each zig and zag will be easier to take in stride.

Transit Tunes

Parents of Impulsive Children are known to check out the location of a bathroom in every place they enter—a store, a restaurant, the mall, a new playmate's house. A speedy response time is usually key to success. As you work on bladder control at home, try a countdown or a song for your child as you're making your way to the bathroom. This will give him something to do on the way to the bathroom, get his mind off his full bladder, and teach him that he needs to try to go to the bathroom sooner.

> ## Potty Talk
>
> **Dad:**   Okay, we've got to get to the bathroom, and I bet we can get there by the time we count to ten, let's go!
>
> Or . . .
>
> **Mom:**   (in fast sing-song voice): This is the way we go to the potty, go to the potty, go to the potty. This is the way we got to the potty, when we have to go!

Eventually you can sing more slowly, or count to twenty or more. At first, parents will probably do most of the talking/singing on the way to the bathroom, which is fine because the point is to distract the child. They should be rushed to the potty at a fast walking clip or even a run. The physical activity may reduce the intensity of the urge to go and the likelihood of an accident. Again, do not regard an accident as failure on your child's part; it is, however, appropriate to try to avoid them.

Follow-through

Over the next year or so, when your Impulsive Child starts a new activity in which she/he becomes absorbed, you may need to remind him of the signs of impending need to go. Pull him away from the activity and quietly suggest he try to go. Reminders are especially needed when the activity is fun. Maintain a matter-of-fact tone when prompting him. Some parents do this well at first but over time lapse into an increasingly frustrated or impatient tone. It can happen to the best of us, but keeping a watchful eye on your own behavior and remembering the personality traits of your child will contribute to good communication, key to teaching him about potty training, or anything else. Be patient. Parents of very Impulsive Kids may find themselves prompting their seven-, eight-, or nine-year-old to remember to use the bathroom on occasion. If you avoid getting frustrated or upset about this, you will save yourself a lot of grief and gray hair, and more importantly, preserve the parent–child relationship.

Similar problems may occur when it's time for your child to focus on learning the more advanced potty skills of effectively wiping and taking the time to wash hands after using the bathroom. Use the techniques that worked earlier: role model the behavior you want them to emulate, reward them with praise and positive encouragement, and explain the benefits of doing it right the first time. At this point, you can explain the finer details of good hygiene. If your child is in daycare or school, it is likely that they're getting these health lessons there. Talk to the teachers and make sure you're using the same language so that you will reaffirm those good habits at home. Continue using statements instead of questions to prompt your child: "You look like you need to use the potty—let's go!" for example.

Nighttime dryness

Once an Impulsive Child has the muscle control for daytime dryness, nighttime dryness might be a fairly smooth transition. The biggest difference in training day versus night for these kids is that at night there are no competing distractions. The unpredictability of their bodily functions will of course still be an issue, so we suggest holding off nighttime potty training until their daytime skills are firmly rooted. As soon as that is established, you can begin the strategies outlined in the Nighttime Dryness section of Chapter 3. The good news is that although Impulsive Children are harder to train initially, the nighttime stuff comes rather quickly compared with the other types of kids.

•••

Potty training the Impulsive Child can feel extremely stressful to some parents. A seemingly neverending cycle of trying to get him to stop what he's doing and try to sit still long enough to go and to solidify any potty successes into his routine. Knowing it's time to go and actually going are two different skills in this child's brain, so parents need to be on top of scheduling, reminding, and redirecting.

This chapter explained the necessity of a routine, as well as the ways in which the Universal Strategies of Role Modeling, Reinforcing Behavior, and Nakedtime will help train Impulsive Children. But the true key lies in the constant reminders from parents, which may have to continue for a long while. Parents should remember that for Impulsive Children, sometimes the urge does come on extremely quickly and thus accidents may be more prevalent with this group. Understanding the way an Impulsive Child's brain works is essential to teaching her anything, and learning that during the potty training age range can be extremely helpful in the years to come.

8

The Strong-Willed Child

Getting inside the minds of Strong-Willed Children can be a rather daunting task, because a fundamental part of their personality is to keep tight control over their thoughts and behaviors. These children don't like to be told what to do and may have unpredictable triggers that can lead to lengthy tantrums. They are slow to adapt to new things that are not of their choosing or of their discovery. Parents of Strong-Willed Kids often feel as if they are walking on eggshells to avoid an outburst. Many parents describe their Strong-Willed Child as stubborn, moody, or inflexible.

In this chapter, parents will learn the art of subtlety, as well as using praise strategically to achieve your goals. Potty training a Strong-Willed Child will often take every available Universal Strategy and sometimes require creative combinations of them. We'll explain why you need to be prepared for some backsliding and, throughout this chapter, we'll remind you how important it is, with these types of children especially, to keep the process stress free.

The Strong-Willed Temperament

Despite being somewhat difficult to deal with now, that strong will is going to serve him or her very well later in life, as adolescents and adults. As you can attest, from their early years, Strong-Willed People know what they want and stay true to their beliefs. With careful nurturing, this trait may translate later to an ability to resist peer pressure—something that's incredibly important and often difficult to come by—during the tween and teen years. Channeled in a positive manner, a strong will can help your child achieve, even surpass, any goal she/he sets. If you are able to potty train your Strong-Willed Child in a thoughtful, caring manner, you will gain lasting valuable parenting skills.

But back to the here and now. When your Strong-Willed Child is involved in an activity of his choice, he tends to be very persistent and attentive. When he wishes to, he can grasp new skills quickly. Because he is resolute in his desires, he may take on leadership roles within his peer group. As long as children of this type feel they are in control, they can be relatively easy to get along with. They are happy, fun-loving, and engaging. They enjoy setting a goal for themselves and reaching it successfully. They take great pride in mastering a talent. They like to be good at things. Once they get it into their head they want to do something, they act much like a Goal-Directed Child who will follow through an activity to its accomplishment. It's the "getting it into their head" part that can be the complex issue. These children work hard when motivated, but when they do not feel invested in the incentive, or feel like they are on someone else's agenda and not their own, they are less likely to work toward the goal.

With Strong-Willed Children, you can show them the hill; you can point out the benefits of going up the hill; you can walk with them to the bottom of the hill and go up the hill yourself; you can call down with a description about how great it is at the top. You can even have the rest of the family go up the hill. But, you can't make the Strong-Willed Child go up the hill until they are ready.

They aren't refusing to go up the hill to spite you. They aren't trying to be difficult (although it may seem that way at times). And it's not always the case that they don't want to go up the hill; they may simply be worried that they'll fall back down. Or they may just want to make their own path on the way up.

Although they may be good at learning new things, they may not feel that way. Some strong-willed behaviors relate to an underlying lack of self-confidence in doing things well. This is similar to the Internalizer who does not want to try something until she feels she can do it perfectly. The Strong-Willed Child often tries to exhibit a sense of total competence, and if she perceives a threat to that competence, she may resist simply because of that underlying insecurity. In other words, if she is being nudged in a direction in which she is not comfortable, her resistance may be more about fear of failing than a desire to be in control.

One of the most frustrating aspects about parenting Strong-Willed Children, especially Strong-Willed Toddlers, is their unpredictable behavior and emotions. Many parents report feeling like they are two steps behind their kids because they don't know what they want and don't know how they're going to react to the next situation. At this age, they don't have the language or comprehension skills to explain why they're behaving a certain way or to ask for help. They may be rather moody and quick to engage in temper tantrums that are more intense and lengthy than those of other kinds of kids. They are slow to adapt to changes, as well, so transitioning from one task to another, or one location to another, can seem fraught with peril. Parents are constantly trying to find ways to make them happy, often without much success. Parents of the Strong-Willed Child, similar to parents of the Sensory-Oriented Child, often find themselves trying to adapt in order to make life more harmonious and easy. However, unlike the Sensory-Oriented Child, for whom a certain amount of adaptation can successfully avert meltdowns, it is very difficult to please the Strong-Willed Child on a consistent basis without completely giving in to his every whim.

Trying to get a Strong-Willed Child to do something he or she doesn't want to do can be likened to "managing up" at your job. It takes creativity and a humble nature. At work, your boss is the one in control and getting credit for every successful idea, but in reality you are putting those great ideas into your boss's head. Now, don't get us wrong, we're not saying that your Strong-Willed Child is the boss of you; however, in order to accomplish a task like potty training, you have to remember that she can do great things when she puts her mind to it. You just want her to think it's all her idea.

It's important for all parents to thoroughly explore their own personality type for compatibility (or possible incompatibility) with their child's traits. This is especially crucial for parents of a Strong-Willed Child. As is the case with other characteristics, personality traits may be genetic. If you also happen to be Strong-Willed, you may butt heads with your child on a regular basis. Guess what? You won't win, especially when it comes to potty training. You'll need to tone down your own need for control and put your child's need first.

If you are an Impulsive Parent with a Strong-Willed Child, be careful not to abandon sound strategies if they don't work immediately. If you do, it'll be like the tail wagging the dog, because the natural tendency is for the child to try to manipulate the parent right back. There is a difference between being a creative and flexible parent who adapts to their child, and being a parent who reacts impulsively to their child's every whim or mood.

Despite your personality type, if you have a Strong-Willed Child, you need to learn to allow him or her to retain control over his or her own bodily functions. You may have already had trouble with sleeping or feeding issues. Remember, no human can force another to eat, sleep, or go to the bathroom. Just because your child has a strong will does not mean you need to break it. You just have to figure out how to effectively channel it.

The Dirty Diaper

In some cases, a Strong-Willed Child will determine he or she is ready to start going on the potty before you are ready. If this happens, watch out! Jeaneane caught her nineteen-month-old daughter Elise sitting on the potty one day with her clothes on. Elise has an older sister who is already potty trained, so it was obvious she was simply copying the behavior. Then Elise started asking to go on the potty, so her mom put her on and she actually peed. Jeaneane thought it was a one-off. But then her "baby" started running to the potty whenever she had to go. This child barely had enough words to explain her needs, and by the most common textbook readiness factors, was not ready to train. But, this Strong-Willed Little Girl was determined! After a week or so, she was taking off her clothes, getting up on the potty, and peeing all on her own! Then she started pooping, too! Too short to be able to reach the sink or move the step stool, Elise still needed a great deal of help with wiping, washing hands, etc., but she was basically potty trained. Jeaneane wasn't ready for this, and at first tried to prevent it from happening. She was shocked (as were all the other jealous moms in her play group!) by Elise's independent streak. But, she ran with it, because she certainly didn't want to prevent her daughter's potty training. Go with the flow (pun intended), is the lesson.

Unfortunately, for most parents, it'll be the other way around; you'll be waiting and waiting for what may seem like forever for your child to show interest. Again, you just have to go with the flow because your Strong-Willed Kid is going to be the one to set the timetable.

The Strong-Willed Child requires an extra level of patience and a relaxed demeanor from the parent in order to best get through the potty training, or any other process. Once you recognize the strong-willed personality trait, and see it from his or her point of view, you will be able to more clearly perceive the reasons behind the intensity, and thus direct his or her natural inclinations toward the goal at hand.

The Art of Subtlety

Parents should take (or fake!) a blasé attitude about the whole thing—no expectations. The more you appear to want or expect your Strong-Willed Child to use the toilet, the more opportunities you are giving your child to frustrate you and control the situation. This is where the Universal Strategy of Keeping Your Perspective is crucial. Similarly, the more you show the Strong-Willed Child that you are willing to get frustrated and upset about the potty-training process, the more you are conveying to him, "Here are my buttons; push them whenever you want."

Parents should remember that they are setting the stage, not getting into a control or power struggle with their child. Parents need to take steps to make it more likely that their kid will ultimately make the decision that potty training is good for him or her, drawing the conclusion that there is some natural—not contrived, not artificial, not parent-driven—incentive for using the potty.

The point is to subtly help these kids realize the benefits of potty training. The kids should discover what's in it for them and think that potty training is their idea. Unless they feel ownership of the goal, they will work hard to maintain the status quo (which they do own) of using diapers.

Keeping timelines and expectations out of potty training will make the process more efficient. If there is a timeline, such as a daycare or a class that requires children to be potty trained by a certain age, then that should be solely a part of your planning, not your child's. Give yourself and your child plenty of time to reach this goal without having that deadline looming over either of you. And, if it seems like you won't meet the deadline, it is your problem to deal with as a parent, not your child's.

Basically, toilet training should be presented as a back-burner goal for the Strong-Willed Child, unless she expresses direct interest. The best actions are subtle attempts to prod her interest, to get her invested in going pee and poop on the toilet. It'll take some careful coaxing and a well thought-out plan to set the stage. Once it is set, you'll need to stand back, give your child some room, and allow her to come to the most logical conclusion—that going on the potty is a worthy adventure to begin!

Potty Dialog

Setting the stage begins way before actual training on the potty. It includes an open dialogue about what, why, when, where, and how you go on the potty. This can begin the moment your child is walking and talking, and doesn't require any action from him or her as yet. Knowledge is power, and your child loves to feel powerful.

As mentioned in Chapter 3, Universal Strategies, one of the most important—and at times overlooked—methods for potty training is simply keeping the bathroom door open when you go about your business. And talk, talk, talk about what's happening in and around the potty. Informational dialog about personal issues is the foundation of a healthy parent–child relationship with benefits that extend beyond potty training.

As with any aspect of parenting, you need to be comfortable with what you are teaching your child; you need to be calm, cool, and collected. If a tactic that we recommend makes you uneasy, by all means skip it and try another. Some people may be too squeamish about their own bathroom behavior to invite total access. If that describes you, bypass the open invitation to the bathroom.

However, when your newly mobile toddler follows you into the bathroom (as they ALL do) and shows curiosity, explain what you're doing in there and why. If you are comfortable to do so, allow him to see what you produce, even flush it down, and compare it to the contents of his diapers. Provide information for as long as he is interested, but let him take the initiative to continue.

When your questioning toddler starts in with the "whys," he will inevitably focus some questions on toilet-related activities. In a non-threatening way, make the point that going on the potty is a big-kid activity.

Potty Talk

Mom: Mommy has to go pee-pee.

Child: Why?

Mom: When I drink water or milk or juice, it goes down my throat, into my tummy, and eventually it will come out as pee-pee into the potty. (Gesturing with your hands down your body as you say this will emphasize the concept.) The same thing happens with food, and that comes out as poop.

Child: Why?

Mom: That's the way our bodies work. Yours does, too. When you drink water or milk or juice, it goes into your mouth, down your throat, into your tummy, and eventually it will come out as pee-pee. (Same gestures.) Right now, your pee-pee and poop go into a diaper, but someday you'll want to try using the potty and then the pee-pee and poop will go in there.

Child: Why?

Mom:	Because that's where big kids and grown-ups make their pee-pee and poop go.
Child:	protesting: But I am a big kid!
Mom:	Yes, and you're getting bigger every day. Pretty soon, you'll be so big you'll want to try going pee-pee and poop on the potty.

Chances are, this will make your child stop the questions to consider that possibility. Many kids, especially the Strong-Willed Ones, aspire to do everything the bigger kids do, so this may pique their curiosity. If they continue with interest and say they want to try, you can put them on the potty (with clothes or without, at their discretion). You could point out their body parts, which you should already have names for, and make this a gentle learning session. You might also show them where their muscles are that have to work to push out the pee-pee and poop. Kids love talking about their muscles! If, by chance, he or she actually has to go at that time, you may have an early victory on your hands. At that juncture, you should give praise in an even-handed way.

Dad: I'm proud of you for trying and, look, you did it! Way to go!

Don't overdo the excitement, or you'll tip them off to how invested you are in their potty success. Don't turn it into a major milestone, and don't say that only babies still wear diapers.

Props

Setting the stage requires props. First, you could try using children's books on the subject. Reading about other children using the potty, and looking at pictures showing what happens, is a nonthreatening way to introduce your child to the idea of going on the toilet. Before you read the book, ask your child what they think the book is about based on the cover. Their answer may give you some insight into their thoughts on the matter.

As you read the book, especially for the first time, stick to the story and be careful not to mention to your child that someday they're going to do this, too. For now, keep everything potty related about the child in the story. Of course, if your child shows interest or asks questions, follow his or her lead and give as much information as requested. Your Strong-Willed Child may just jump right up from reading the story and ask if she or he can try it, too!

The first potty-related book could be read at the library or borrowed from a friend to find out how it's received before you spend the money for one. Otherwise, you could get one and place it on the bookshelf to let your child "find" it. This may pique their interest more naturally than if you suggest it. If you choose this route, feigning surprise and asking your child to help you figure out what this "mystery" book is all about is a good way to give your child control of the situation.

If your Strong-Willed Child resists reading a book about the potty, don't push it. Other props such as videos and dolls may come across as contrived with a Strong-Willed Child. However, many storybooks have accompanying videos, and if your child expresses interest in the book, give the video a try. Again, if you encounter resistance, shelve the video for now.

Dolls can be a terrific tool to show your children the mechanics of toileting. You can show them about the what, where, and how, but explain that dolls don't always have the same body parts that real people have. For Strong-Willed Children, we suggest skipping the special "Potty-Training Dolls" on the market. The regular dolls that come with a pretend potty and can make pretend pee-pee might be a more natural introduction to the topic. If your kid isn't usually interested in dolls, however, omit them, especially if yours is a boy who doesn't have any other dolls. Don't misunderstand us on this point—it's not that boys cannot use a potty-training doll; it's simply that a Strong-Willed Boy who does not have any other dolls will likely see this as attempted manipulation.

First Steps

Role Modeling

When you're ready to start the potty-training process in earnest, step up your modeling behavior. Instead of simply allowing your child to follow and watch you, you should begin to speak more specifically about the when, where, and why of going on the toilet. Call attention to your own potty breaks, provide an explanation of what you're doing, and then casually ask if she/he wants to give it a try. Present it as just another incidental part of everyone's day. Try to anticipate the things your child may not like about potty training and talk about how you deal with those issues. For example, if you think your son will hate having to stop a favorite activity when he has to go, invent that kind of situation for yourself first and talk about it. You may feel silly, but a little acting can give you the opportunity to speak your thoughts out loud and avoid directing the words to him:

> *Dad (as if talking to himself): Uh-oh, I've got to go pee-pee! Ugh, I don't want to stop playing baseball, but if I don't the pee-pee will come out all over me. I'd better stop and go inside to the bathroom, and then I can come back real quick and keep playing.*

Later on, if/when your Strong-Willed Son doesn't want to stop playing to go potty, you have a perfect opportunity to remind him that everyone has to do that from time to time. In the meantime, after your narration, your child's natural curiosity may well carry him right into the bathroom with you, which gives you the perfect opportunity to capitalize. You should continue to talk out loud to yourself about what you are doing.

> *Dad: Oh, good, I'm here, I've really got to go! I'm going to pull down my pants, point, and . . . here's the pee-pee coming out!*

Your child will be watching closely, and may even peer around you to get a better look at what you're doing. If this makes you uncomfortable, you don't have to grant this much access, but be careful not to get angry at your child's interest. A simple, matter-of-fact statement about privacy will suffice to get him to step away and to begin the larger lesson of privacy.

> *Dad: Hey buddy, step back a little, please, and give me some space. Going pee-pee and poop in the potty is something you'll learn to do just like Daddy someday, but these parts of our bodies are private. Do you know what private means? It means it's not for anyone else to look at or touch. It's okay a little bit, because I'm showing you how to go pee-pee in the potty, but you shouldn't get so close.*

Regardless of the amount of access you allow, when you talk about your child learning these toileting skills, don't express a timeline expectation. Keep it loose and strictly informational; a timeline or deadline will put too much pressure on your child at this early juncture, and make her feel like this is your goal instead of hers. Sometimes Acting Like a Coach, unless you're very careful about it, can have the same effect. You don't want to turn her off before she even gets started.

At least at first, it is best to model along gender lines—Moms teach daughters and Dads teach sons—whenever possible. This does not mean that Moms can't teach boys or Dads their girls, but keep this in mind: Strong-Willed Children in particular will want to do it exactly the way you did, so if Dad pees standing up, that's what your child may want to do. With boys, it's not that big of a deal, but it is easier to start them off sitting down even for pee. A girl trying to pee standing up (yes, they will try it!) is not going to be successful and this will not be the best start for the potty-training process.

Think ahead about how you will teach the details of using the toilet. For instance, if you fold the toilet paper to wipe, a Strong-Willed child will too, forever. And, not having the dexterity or practice of an adult, she/he may spend a long time trying to fold it exactly like Mom or Dad. (This may drive a Strong-Willed Parent who wads the paper bonkers, by the way!) A Strong-Willed Child, if they are ready, will take the first lesson deep into the heart and psyche, so make sure you think about all the steps involved first and teach it the way you want it done the first time.

Modeling behavior can come from older siblings, playmates, and even pets. Obviously, if your Strong-Willed Child sees siblings and friends that she looks up to doing it, she may want to imitate the behavior. Strong-Willed Kids really like to keep up with, or stay ahead of, others. This form of peer pressure is a built-in bonus for daycare potty training; everyone else in the class is doing it, so your child will want to as well. At home, however, watching another child go to the bathroom may be a touchy subject for that child or his parents. If it's your own child, make sure they are comfortable letting little brother or sister observe. If you are friendly with another child's family and the kids are around the same age, having the child who's further ahead in potty training show off their skills can be all the incentive your Strong-Willed Child needs to get serious. Ask permission from the child's parent ahead of time. If the other child balks at having an audience, back off—you don't want to be responsible for derailing your friend's potty-training efforts with her child!

Making any part of the potty-training process familiar will stimulate your child's interest, and even a discussion of your pet's potty habits can contribute. Pets often "ask" to go out—dogs scratch and cats meow at the door. Observing a pet peeing or pooping teaches that these behaviors are not random. Cats are very good for this, because they take great care to cover what they've produced, and they go through the same motions each time. Housebroken dogs may also be a good example. For both, there is a specific place they go, just like people. Outdoor dogs may be less fastidious and therefore an inferior example. Nonetheless, helping your child understand that every living thing has to pee and poop will be the valuable lesson.

At this early point, don't personalize these lessons too much. Strong-Willed Children will listen carefully when you critique someone else, but they don't like a critique of their own behavior. You can comment on other people's children, as long as they're random strangers, for example in a store or walking in front of you down the street, but make sure the strangers can't hear you discussing them.

Mom: Look, honey, see that girl up there? She looks like she's about your age and I can see she's not wearing a diaper! I'll bet she's learned how to use the potty just like you're doing.

It is fine to comment on the kids that are potty trained as well as those who are not. Strong-Willed Kids like to feel superior, so pointing out an older child who is not potty trained is okay. But do this judiciously, because you don't want the sticky situation whereby your child repeats any of your comments back to a friend or daycare peer! Avoid using shame, such as suggesting your child isn't doing a good enough job compared with the random girl you just pointed out. This will not further your cause with a Strong-Willed Child.

Praise, Praise, Praise Their Efforts

Positive reinforcement is very important with a Strong-Willed Child. In a broad sense, this is a method by which a desired behavior is made more likely to occur in the future. It is one of the most important kinds of parenting tools, used to encourage continued work in many different circumstances. Strong-Willed Children crave positive attention, and they like everything to be about them. Kids like to believe they are good at things, and positive reinforcement is a direct way to communicate that a child is achieving competence. Positive feedback is encouraging and empowering. Tie your praise closely to the action, underscore the fact that the accomplishment is your child's (as opposed to yours), and refrain from upping the expectations the instant progress is made.

Some kids like their parents to display very excited reactions to their successes, whereas others, including many Strong-Willed Children, will view these as phony. Positive reinforcement must be personalized to the child. A useful kind of praise for Strong-Willed Kids is to be "surprised" by their performance. Here is an example:

> *Mom: You mean you are only 2 years old (or 3 years old or whatever the case may be) and you are starting to use the potty?! Wow!! I really don't know that many kids who are only 2 (or 3) who can use the potty like that! I am really impressed!*

These kids love thinking they are better at doing things than other people. Feel free to share these lines with other influential adults in your child's life—grandparents, neighbors, daycare providers. Impressing your parents is one thing, but most kids instinctively know that's pretty easy to do. Enlisting outside praise will reinforce your Strong-Willed Child's feeling that this is a special accomplishment.

You can also layer your praise, which is especially useful over time. For example, after your son or daughter has been peeing on the potty successfully for a while, you might start to primarily praise his wiping technique or consistent handwashing while secondarily noting the continued great job of peeing.

Dad: Wow! You're doing such a great job using the toilet paper. Not only can you pee-pee in the potty by yourself, but now you can wipe all by yourself, too? You are amazing! I wonder what new thing you'll learn to do tomorrow?

Although you should refrain from making potty training the total focus, use praise liberally with a Strong-Willed Child. Give examples. Don't manipulate or scold alongside praise (avoid the "That was good, but . . ." kind of statements), but praise unconditionally. Give kudos for trying, too, not just when pee or poop is produced.

Mom: You did a good job sitting here for a minute and trying, even though nothing came out. Next time, maybe it will.

Candy or toys are a bit of manipulation that your Strong-Willed Child will exploit as far as possible, until they eventually outright reject it. The natural tendency of this type of child is to manipulate "the system" right back, so you may find yourself promising and purchasing more and more rewards for each and every behavior. If you're starting to feel like potty training has become an expensive endeavor, you may have fallen into this trap.

Much more effective tactics, for the short and long term, are modeling, praise, and the powerful feeling of success your child will get from the accomplishment of the goal. These are stronger motivators for a Strong-Willed Child, and will stimulate the internal process of deciding for herself that it is a worthwhile adventure. If rewards garner a quick response from your child and you do want to continue with that, better choices than the latest toy are prizes like choosing her own big-kid underwear imprinted with her favorite character or being able to attend a special big-kid activity because she no longer has to wear a diaper. Tie any reward or incentive to the potty training and use it as a natural consequence of her efforts to go on the potty.

If you've already started offering tangible rewards and your child has come to expect them, it's probably not going to help your cause to stop cold turkey, so ease into the other incentives. Spin it as a way for them to take potty training to the next level.

Potty Talk

Dad: Now that you're really getting the hang of going pee-pee on the potty, it's time you picked out your own kind of big boy/girl underwear. I saw some at the store the other day—they had (insert favorite character's name) on them. Do you think you'd like them?

Child: Yeah!!

Dad: Okay, then, what we need to do is to start learning how to go poop in the potty. These are really special underwear that we don't want to get messed up, So as soon as you get good at pooping into the potty just like you are with pee-pee, then we'll go to the store. I can't wait for you to get them—they are really cool!

The emphasis here is on the child's desire for the underwear, a natural consequence that is directly related to successful pooping. It is presented in a way that does not emphasize your control of the reward. Rather, you are your child's biggest supporter of eventually getting the new underwear. Although you do control access to the reward, and you are using the possibility of the reward as an incentive to stimulate motivation, your desire to influence the child's behavior is not highlighted. Instead, your child is getting to choose something cool, and you convey that you want that as much as your child. It is a fine line, but this dialog is much different than saying, "As soon as you learn to poop on the potty, we'll get you the underwear."

Capitalize on Every Opportunity

Observe carefully and capitalize on each moment that your Strong-Willed Child shows interest or curiosity in using the potty. If she expresses a desire to take a step forward in the process—perhaps she wants to wear big-kid underpants or no longer wear diapers—you can use this as an opportunity to focus more directly. Because it was her idea in the first place (which parents can subtly work into their statements), the Strong-Willed Child may be willing to work harder and more directly on the goal.

Not only is this an opportunity to start training, but because it was your child's idea, you are insulated from the suspicion of setting the agenda. It is perfectly acceptable to gently remind your Strong-Willed Child that potty training was his idea in the first place.

Potty Talk

Mom: Remember when you said you wanted to learn to use the potty? I know some ways that can help.

Or . . .

Dad: I think it is a great idea that you want to learn to use the potty and I will help you any way that I can!

Be careful of the fine line between capitalizing on an opening and making a big issue of it. If you've been thwarted in your efforts, back off and ignore potty training for a while. Don't throw their earlier interest back in their face. In fact, it's best not to mention it at all. They had interest once and they will again. If you use other subtle means to encourage interest, they'll come back to it when they're ready. If your child is near 3½ years, we're willing to bet that it will happen before too long.

Nakedtime

Nakedtime is one of our suggested first steps in Chapter 3, Universal Strategies. Nonthreatening and novel, it works exceedingly well with Strong-Willed Children because there is no doubt about who is in control of your child's bodily functions. Your child will get firsthand experience in feeling the control.

Most children react well to the suggestion that they run around naked all day. They love it. However, with a Strong-Willed Child, if something happens to take the shine off this newfound activity, such as a fall from the swing set or a sunburn, she may turn against it with a vengeance. Think carefully about how you will go about nakedtime and read through our safety suggestions in Chapter 3 to ensure your child does not experience discomfort while trying it out.

If you've been monitoring your kid's regular schedule of eliminating, try doing nakedtime when he is more likely to actually have to pee. You can also give him an extra cup of water before and during the naked sessions to help his bladder along; this is especially easy and healthy to do if it's hot and you're doing it outside. We suggest not trying nakedtime during the period of time your child normally poops. Mastering pee-pee should be the first lesson in potty training. Do not present nakedtime as an activity connected with potty training. Simply offer it as something funny, different, or, if you have house rules about wearing clothes, a special exemption from the normal rule.

When your son or daughter first pees during nakedtime, you'll probably have to point it out. He or she may not notice that it is happening until she feels it trickle down his or her legs. Many children will be upset by this, and you should react with the same calm, relaxed demeanor you have when talking about anything potty related. For example:

Potty Talk

Child: Daddy, there's some wet stuff all over my legs!

Dad: Wow, you just went pee-pee. That's okay. Let's get you all cleaned up and then we can play some more.

If your child follows up on this short explanation with any questions, do your best to explain things honestly.

Child: But I didn't want to go pee-pee. How come I went pee-pee?

Dad: I think you had so much pee-pee inside that it just had to come out. It's okay; it happens to everyone. Since you don't have a diaper on, the pee-pee came out everywhere. Grown-ups don't wear diapers; we go to the potty when we have to go and we put our pee-pee in there and then flush it away. Do you want to try that next time?

Child: Yes.*

Dad: Okay, so next time you feel like you have to go pee-pee, tell me and we'll run really really fast, like a race, to get to the potty. Does that sound like a good plan to you?

*Alternate scenario, Child: No! I don't want to!

Dad: That's okay. Maybe someday you'll want to. Right now, let's get you all cleaned up.

Keep your explanations brief and to the point. You could explain that you and all the other family members that your child sees going to the bathroom on a regular basis—grandparents, older siblings, your spouse—use the toilet this way, and they had to learn when they were around his age too. It shouldn't sound too much like a "lesson." You could inject something silly to make him laugh, or encourage him to ask other family members how they learned to use the potty. Be sure to warn them ahead of time and coach them on the ways you'd like them to handle the subject.

If at any time your child balks, simply respond with, "That's okay," and drop the subject. This will enable you to maintain the no-expectations façade, and will reassure your child that this is not an agenda he's being manipulated into.

With the Strong-Willed Child, you may have to wade through a handful of messy nakedtime sessions before you see the first inkling of interest. She may be suspicious of your motives and test whether you're trying to force the issue. She may have some latent Sensory-Oriented or Internalizing personality traits that surface during these sessions, so we suggest you read through those chapters too. Hopefully, though, she will decide to put her mind toward mastering this skill and you'll be well on your way.

If, after a number of nakedtime sessions, your Strong-Willed Child is still refusing your invitation to try the potty, ease back and throw another subtle tactic into the mix. It's not necessary to abandon these sessions all together, because some children will take a good long time to decide they want to start. But if you're tired of cleaning up after your little pooper, it is fine to put nakedtime on hold; you can revisit this strategy if a more appropriate time presents itself.

Do not put restrictions on the sessions if nakedtime does not immediately work (for example, "We can only do nakedtime when you start using the potty"). An exception would be if your little boy starts to purposefully "spray" the area for fun, in which case you may need to institute some rules. Determine where they got this idea—sometimes they start on their own, but possible suspects are older boys or television shows—and put a stop to it. If this happens, you can be assured that he must have a good handle on the mechanics of elimination, and you can use this to your advantage.

> *Mom: Well, I can see you sure know how to control your pee-pee, but spraying it all over the bathroom/yard is not okay. It makes a big mess and spreads germs. Let's get this all cleaned up and next time I'd like you to show me how you can make it go right into the potty.*

If you haven't tried the Cheerios in the toilet for aim practice, now's the time to try it. The cereal pieces float, make excellent targets, and are flushable. You could also put some food coloring in the toilet water for the first few times and challenge him to make it change color.

Nakedtime has the potential to get ugly. Some naked children may play with their poop or pee and even go to their mouth with it. Of course, this will understandably fire up a parent, some of whom may yell out to stop the behavior, which sets in motion the type of power struggle that we have advised in this entire book to avoid. The best course of action is to restrict or eliminate nakedtime sessions. They no longer serve the purpose of potty training; instead, they are being used for fun or to press a parent's buttons, and this will only set the process back.

Accidents

When Strong-Willed Children decide to embark on their potty-training journey, their biggest concern will be maintaining control. They want to control the agenda, the timing, the acquisition of skills, and the decision to tackle a new skill. Having an accident cuts straight to the heart of their concern—they were not able to control their body and even worse their "mistake" is on display! It can be very stressful for these children to come to terms with an accident. Some will double their efforts; others will be demoralized.

As a caring parent, you'll want to make sure that you prepare your child for the eventuality of an accident during the time you're setting the stage for potty training. If they know what might happen, it's not such a big surprise when it does. A good time to do this is during the narration of your role modeling. You could comment as an aside that accidents happen to everyone and that's just a normal part of learning.

Dad: Boy, I really had to go bad! I'm glad I made it to the potty on time. I remember a few times when I was little and I didn't get there before the pee-pee came out. Instead of putting it into the potty, the pee-pee went all over my pants. I was really sad, but my mommy—Grandma—helped me and I was okay. Everyone has accidents sometimes, it's no big deal.

In order for your child to have absolute trust in your support, you're going to have to follow through and keep calm in reaction to an accident. If you yell or otherwise overreact when he has an accident—even if it's all over the seat of the car or on an expensive rug—this will resonate within the Strong-Willed Child and short-circuit any progress you've already made.

Praise should be given even after an accident, because expressions of disappointment or frustration will undermine all your teachings thus far. Find something positive about the situation and focus your words on that. Don't sugarcoat unnecessarily, as your Strong-Willed Toddler or Preschooler is on the lookout for blatant manipulation, but you do need to find a way to bolster self-esteem while acknowledging the truth of an accident. Here's one way to do this.

Potty Talk

Child: Mommy, I had an accident!

Mom: Okay, sweetie, thanks for telling me. It's all right, that happens to everyone when they're learning how to go on the potty. I'm glad you realized it and told me right away so we can get you cleaned up. I'll bet you came really close to stopping that pee-pee before it came out . . . you'll be able to do it next time. You're getting the hang of all this so fast! I think it took me a lot longer when I was a little girl.

Accentuate the positive, keep your tone neutral or upbeat, and express the confidence you have in your child that she may not have in herself at this moment. Remind yourself of your own temperament at this time, as well. If you find that you are fussing at your daughter about accidents, or getting into power struggles about sitting on the potty to try, then perhaps ignoring accidents will be a better tactic. For Strong-Willed Kids, more so than others, drawing attention to the negative behavior over which they hold all control is not going to get you anywhere. Keep in mind that your child doesn't enjoy having accidents, and in her own time she will learn better bladder control. You need to have the will to step back and give her the room to figure it out on her own.

Backsliding

Being a bit more controlling, now that he's started the process, is acceptable at this point. You need to make sure he realizes you're unswerving and will hold him to what he's learned. Do not allow your child to slide back into pretraining mode. Above all, during training, do not schedule any activity that could be ruined by an accident, such as a long trip, birthday party, or family vacation. Avoid the big scene where you end up losing your temper with your child over toileting. Negative interaction patterns spill over into other issues, often get worse over time, and can be really hard to change as the child gets older. Training a Strong-Willed Child is never a picnic, but this is the first battle of many to be fought.

Once your son or daughter has shown a pretty good capacity to control their elimination, teach them that the natural consequence of the accomplishment is no more diapers! Nighttime control may continue to be an issue for some time, so the use of a training diaper at night is not a big deal. Using a diaper during the day, however, should no longer be an option. This can be a gradual process. After she goes pee on the potty, let her wear underwear for the next two hours, then gradually increase the time as she gets better at holding it. Or, you can choose to make the transition permanent on a particular day. But once the diapers are gone, they are gone for good, and your child should know that. If there are no diapers in the house, then they are not an option. Or if the pull-on diapers are locked in the "nighttime box" that can only be opened at bedtime, then they are not an option during the day. All this will facilitate forward movement in the toilet training and avoid the chance of a power struggle about when a diaper is used.

Continue moving forward, however slowly it goes. Refer back to the sequence of skill acquisitions in Chapter 2, page 26, to determine what comes next. Accomplishing each step is a success. Treat it as such in your own mind, but don't let on to your Strong-Willed Child that it means so much to you. He should see you as a helper in this process. Otherwise, he is in control of his own destiny.

Potty Rules

Lay out the rules for going potty from the beginning: flushing the toilet every time, washing hands afterward, putting the lid back down. Use the techniques in the Universal Strategy of Giving Good Directions to ensure your child understands the rules you have in place. Whatever your house rules are, your child should know them and abide by them. Get your spouse on the same page with you or you'll get resistance from your child. Of course, don't make the process of using the potty unpleasant simply because the child didn't do a very good job of washing hands afterward. This could cause the Strong-Willed Child to interrupt the successful process simply because of the negative feedback from some peripheral behavior. That said, each of these learned behaviors will likely require some of the same careful coaxing as the act of peeing on the potty did. Additionally, set a good example. Families who model good hygiene and cleanliness will be showing the newly trained child the right habits.

This is a time to choose your battles carefully and be creative. If your Strong-Willed Son or Daughter is going on the potty and is out of diapers, this is a big success. With that in mind, you'll need to ask yourself whether issues such as not wiping well or not washing hands effectively are worth fighting over. If he forgets to put the seat up when peeing, have him help clean up afterward. If he doesn't wash his hands very well, keep some hand sanitizer close by. If he doesn't wipe real well but at least makes an attempt, let him know that you'll take care of the final wipe. Make sure your child at least tries to wipe; some parents are too quick to take over and are then surprised and frustrated when their six- or seven-year-old continues to demand help wiping after every poop.

To lend support to your decisions, you could get your pediatrician involved. It may be hard for a parent of a Strong-Willed Child to believe, but these kids usually don't act strong-willed to everyone, and she/he may be remarkably respectful toward an authority figure. It's perfectly acceptable to ask your doctor to address potty training directly with your child at his or her third-year check-up. Coach the doctor on the tactic you're taking and discuss ways he or she can help it along. The pediatrician could simply tell your three-year-old that it is time to start sitting on the potty every day or that pretty soon it'll be time to start wearing big-kid underpants. Strong-Willed Children might be quick to follow instructions given by the doctor, even if the child has been indifferent toward or actively resisted those very same directions from you, the parent. Reminding your child what the doctor said is a good way to start a conversation about potty training.

Advanced Skills

As your Strong-Willed Child masters the basic skills of potty training, you can continue to refer back to the Acquisition of Skills chart in Chapter 2, page 26, to see what skill is up next. Because it happens less often, pooping into the potty is generally considered a more advanced skill, as is wiping the poop. If you've been taking it one step at a time, you've likely ignored the pooping skills in favor of getting your child's peeing habits firmly established. But if she's dry all day, having fewer accidents, and has a good grasp of going pee-pee in the potty, you're ready to move forward.

At this point, you should assess whether your child is ready to tackle pooping. Remember to use positive reinforcement language. A good time to approach the subject is just after they've peed, while they are still sitting on the potty.

Potty Talk

Dad: You are so great at going pee-pee on the potty now, son! I'm proud of you. Do you think you'd like to learn about the muscles you use for pooping on the potty?

Child: Yes.*

> **Dad:** Great! Pooping is the next thing for big boys to learn. So, what most people do is while they're sitting on the potty after going pee-pee, they try to use their other muscles to see if there is any poop to push out. How about you try that right now, see if you can push!
>
> *Alternate Scenario, if the child responds with "No!"
>
> **Dad:** That's okay. Now that you're pee-peeing in the potty really well, poop is the next thing to learn. But you don't have to learn that today. Maybe you'll want to try pooping next time.

As before, keep your expectations on the back burner, give your child time to consider it, and be vocal about role modeling your own bowel activity. You can use the same tactics you used earlier, amended for the solid form of elimination instead of the liquid. Do keep in mind that your child's fears and frustrations will likely be a little different. When successes come, use the former positive reinforcement techniques of praise and the incentive of attending more big-kid activities after he or she has mastered this skill.

Strong-Willed Children are more willing than other personality types to put up with some discomfort simply to maintain control. For this reason, you need to be watchful for constipation. Withholding stools is a common problem for all kinds of children, but control is more at issue for Strong-Willed Kids. If they don't feel in control of their own body, they'll take control, even if it means hijacking their own bodily functions. Children who are asserting their rights have often tried other avenues first, such as complaining, excusing behavior, having a lot of accidents when you think they're beyond that, teasing others, and withholding for longer amounts of time. Constipation can become chronic, and very painful, so prompt attention from parents and a pediatrician are needed. You can read more about the problem of constipation in Chapter 10. This should serve to reinforce the value of avoiding a power struggle with your child.

That resolute need to remain in control can manifest itself in other ways. Some Strong-Willed Children will not be forthcoming about accidents. If you find soiled underwear wadded up under the bed or hidden in the toy box, for example, your child is sending a signal that she/he is afraid of admitting to you that they have failed. Creating or renewing a relaxed and comfortable interaction will lead to a greater willingness on his or her part to share.

Don't put overt pressure on your Strong-Willed Son or Daughter to get pooping down as well as he or she has mastered peeing. Your child may feel cornered if the expectations are too heavy. If a parent is confident that their child is not feeling overly pressured, then the reasonable response to hidden dirty underwear might be to have the child assist with the clean-up. The underwear will probably need to be washed out before usual laundering. This type of consequence does not need to be delivered as a punishment or with any judgment or implied message. Instead, be very matter-of-fact and direct about consequences for actions.

Mom: You dirtied the underwear so now you have to help me clean everything up. It's okay to have an accident, but it is not okay for you to hide your poopy underwear so I can't find them. Poop has germs and those germs could have been spread onto your bed (or toys, whatever was near the hiding place). Let's wash out these undies and put them in the washing machine. Next time, please tell me when you've had an accident and I'll help you.

In this situation, it may be tempting to simply throw the dirty underwear away and buy new ones; however, this will only serve to enable the behavior. Frank discussion with your child, closer supervision, and a reduction in your expectations are more likely to produce the results you want.

Nothing's Working?

Sometimes there is just nothing you can do to spark the urge to potty train in Strong-Willed Children. If the impetus isn't there, it is probably best to put the idea on the back burner for a while. Continue to use—but not in an "in-your-face" manner—modeling behaviors, props such as books if they are still well received, and passive training techniques such as nakedtime, as much as possible. Keep potty training in the background of your life, let your child know that she can return to it at any time, but do not make her think you're waiting with bated breath for that day to come. With many other kinds of children, there are ways to move the process forward despite reluctance; trying this with a Strong-Willed child, however, will only entrench his refusal. Above all, never force children of this personality type to do anything with regard to potty training. That will only serve to double or triple your child's efforts to refuse to go in the potty. Keep in mind that most children will kick into potty training by age 3½, especially if they're around peers on a regular basis.

The best way to train your Strong-Willed Kid is to allow them to potty train at a slow pace. We know it's hard to wait for them to make up their mind, but you'll both benefit by their success once they are ready!

•••

Control is the key word to keep in mind when dealing with a Strong-Willed Child. As with many of the other types of children described in this book, what you learn from the potty-training process will go a long way toward shaping their future behavior, while keeping a healthy and happy parent–child relationship intact. It is essential when potty training a Strong-Willed Child that you let them think that going in the potty is their own idea. Slow to adapt, these kids need to want to change their behavior in order for the process to be successfully completed. A huge dose of patience is crucial—take (or fake!) a blasé attitude about the whole thing.

The Universal Strategies of Role Modeling, Positive Reinforcement and Nakedtime are likely to be your best bets. Capitalize on every opportunity that comes your way and avoid backsliding by continually moving forward to the next skill that needs to be learned. Set out your potty rules from the very beginning and stick to them no matter what. At the same time, remember that just because your child has a strong will does not mean you need to break it. You just have to learn to channel it in the right direction.

9

Common Interruptions

Regardless of your child's dominant personality type, whether it is Goal-Directed, Sensory-Oriented, Internalizing, Impulsive, or Strong-Willed, you can count on an interruption or two during the learning process. Just when you think potty training is on a roll, your child may get sick, or it'll take longer than expected and run into a planned vacation or a move. Hopefully, you'll have planned potty training around the arrival of a new baby, but . . . well, we know things don't always go as planned when you have children.

So, how should you handle these kinds of situations? The short answer is that you want to react to an interruption in the same way you would to an accident—in a relaxed and matter-of-fact way, with consideration for your child's mindset.

In this chapter, we walk you through some of the most common types of interruptions. Remember, this book is all about taking the stress out of potty training, and that stress level is at its highest when you're derailed after thinking you were speeding toward the finish line. Interruptions can be supremely stressful for you as a parent, but also for your child, whose self-confidence is still shaky.

Illness

If your child starts feeling sick during potty training, you'll need to carefully adjust your schedule and training techniques based on his or her symptoms. For example, the sniffles or a cold might not affect the process that much, but a fever can sap your child's energy and make it difficult to try often or react quickly when needed. Be prepared for, and be forgiving of, more accidents while they are feeling sick. Make sure that you link the additional accidents to their illness in words familiar to your children, so they understand that they aren't doing anything wrong.

However, a bacteria or viral infection can cause diarrhea and that will have a huge impact on your training. Your child's ability to understand the signals of impending diarrhea will be greatly compromised, not to mention the impossibility of controlling his or her rectal muscles at this point. In particular, diarrhea can be demoralizing, especially for Sensory-Oriented, Strong-Willed, and Internalizing Children. Goal-Directed Kids will also be upset at the setback, but most will probably listen when you explain that it's just temporary. Strong-Willed Kids may be angry because they can't control their bowels anymore. But both Goal-Directed and Strong-Willed Children will likely be able to pick up where they left off. Sensory-Oriented Children will be extremely distressed by the aches, pains, and mess, whereas Internalizers will interpret the accidents as a major failure on their part. Both Sensory-Oriented and Internalizers will likely need to be eased back into potty training, probably from an earlier point in the process.

If it's a very bad case of diarrhea, and it is adversely affecting your child's confidence, you may want to consider using the "nighttime" diapers for a short-term solution. If your child is more than 3 years old, you'll have to do some explaining.

Mom: Aw, sweetheart, I'm sorry you're sick. I know it's really hard to keep the diarrhea from getting all over your underwear. You're doing a great job trying to go in the potty, but your body has a lot of germs it's trying to get rid of—that's what the diarrhea is, germs—and it's coming out too fast to get it into the potty. So let's put you in one of your nighttime training diapers just for today and maybe tomorrow if you still have diarrhea like this.

We've said in other chapters that once you make the transition to diapers you should not go back. However, during a bad bout of diarrhea, you run the risk of doing more damage to the potty-training process by letting your child become discouraged than by relapsing temporarily to diapers. In this instance, you need to make the less risky choice based on your specific situation.

During an illness, Impulsive Kids often show a secondary personality trait; they'll perhaps internalize or become sensory oriented, though you might also see a little strong will. Impulsive children are the "forgive-and-forget" type; the forgetting part, however, is concerning. After their illness, they may not have the same commitment to potty training (and even then it probably wasn't that much), so your challenge will be to build their motivation back up.

Vacation

When you start potty training in earnest, pick a time during which you have no immediate vacation plans. Of course, teaching your child how to go on the toilet can sometimes take a great deal longer than you've planned. If it runs into a vacation, you're going to have to gauge your child's progress, weigh the particulars of your itinerary, and then muddle through as best you can. We'll give you a couple of scenarios to, hopefully, illustrate the different issues you should consider. Be sure to pack plenty of extra changes of clothes wherever you're traveling, because there will most likely be some added accidents.

If you are vacationing at a hotel in a family-friendly place, such as Disneyworld, the good news is that most theme parks are chockfull of bathrooms, simply because of the sheer number of families that visit. If you are going with another family whose children are already trained, they could role model potty behavior for your child.

Sometimes a change of location is not a big deal for a child, although some kids are scared of unfamiliar potties or the automatic flush toilets that are prevalent at theme parks. A possible benefit is that you have some fantastic incentive opportunities to discuss with your child, and the excitement of the park may be enough to spur your child past any fears or anxieties. Simply put, your child's mind will be elsewhere, so capitalize on that! However, your child will likely be overstimulated and overtired, and thus it'll be harder for them to concentrate on going potty.

Long trips in a car or airplane can also be challenging, so ramp up the "trying" behavior ahead of time. If you are driving, consider bringing along your potty chair for easier pit stops. Hotel stays can go both ways. Be sure to ask for a waterproof liner for the bed, or bring one of your own, as your child is likely to be more tired and less able to wake up in the night to go to the bathroom. Make sure to leave a light on in the bathroom, which will cut down on navigational problems in the middle of the night.

Heading to Grandma and Grandpa's house for vacation? You can likely continue potty training as you've been doing, provided you clear it with Grandma and Grandpa first. After all, it is their house that will suffer the consequences of an accident. If they're the type to get angry at a potty-training child getting pee-pee on the carpets, consider staying at a nearby hotel instead. Again, bringing along your own potty chair could be helpful and more relaxing for your child—especially if Grandma and Grandpa still have that old green toilet! Hopefully, your child is already familiar with the layout of their home. However, if not, do a few practice sessions running to the bathroom from the spot where your child will be sleeping. Leave a light on in the bathroom, or bring a nightlight with you. Above all, don't allow your parents or in-laws to shame or force your child into anything they aren't ready for. This will not help your efforts.

Did you book a trip to some exotic, out of the way locale? Well, we certainly applaud your optimism and the fact that you've retained a sense of adventure after having children. However, if you can get your money back, consider rescheduling this kind of vacation. Long trips of any kind are tough on little kids, but the difficulty becomes extreme (for kids and parents) in unknown territory, perhaps in a foreign country, where nothing is remotely familiar to your child. Couple this with the possibility of traveler's diarrhea, and you have the makings of a disaster or, at the very least, some unhappy memories of a stressful trip.

If you can't reschedule, contact the tour operators, airlines, hotels, or any other organization through which you've booked your trip and ask what types of child-friendly services they have available. Ask how accessible bathrooms will be at any stop along the way. Again, we suggest packing both a waterproof bed liner for nights as well as a smaller waterproof pad for travel and naps, along with plenty of wipes!

Moving or Going to a New School

Moving your home or starting at a new daycare or school can leave your child feeling as if the solid foundation of his or her life is a bit wobbly. It probably goes without saying, but you need to consider your child's personality and temperament before deciding how to proceed. You'll also need to consider how far you've progressed into potty training to determine if it's more worthwhile to continue or to interrupt it temporarily. Either way, your choice should be based on what's best for your child.

Although it may seem that going back into diapers would be the less stressful choice at this time for children just in the beginning of the process, this decision undermines the self-confidence that potty training has brought to some of them. In many cases, continuing the activities you were doing before this change is the best choice. A pause in potty training simply means that you maintain the status quo. Wait until your child adjusts to the new situation before moving forward with training in new skills.

Again, it all depends on the particulars of your situation, but the most compassionate way to deal with this may simply be to step back and let your child take the lead. Whatever direction the child heads in, you should willingly follow.

New Baby

It's no secret that toddlers sometimes take the attitude that a new baby in the family is an invader into their territory. For these children, the arrival of baby can throw a wrench into potty training, as the circumstances of their lives and places in the family changes. Even though you and your spouse may be overjoyed at your new addition, try to remember a time when you were thrown off by change and then keep that experience in your mind when dealing with your older children.

When a new sibling enters the picture, a child in the midst of potty training may regress to an earlier point in the process. For that reason, you need to be talking about the new baby and your child's potty-training skills in the time leading up to the baby's arrival. Your aim is to make sure your child is sure of your love, has self-confidence in his potty training successes, and understands that a new baby won't take his place.

Double-down on the Universal Strategy of Being a Potty Role Model in the month before the baby is due. Talk, talk, and talk about the kinds of tasks you'll be doing with the baby: feedings, changings, naps. Hopefully, you'll have the baby's space ready to go, and you can couple Role Modeling with Practice Sessions so your child to learn what it will be like for her to go potty while you are caring for the baby.

Foe example, carry a doll or a stuffed animal with you. Pretend to be changing the doll/baby and not being able to stop to bring your child to the bathroom. This is a great way to help him or her practice holding it for a short period of time. Doing some Practice Sessions in advance with scenarios like this will allow your child to become comfortable with the idea of going into the bathroom and going potty alone (provided your child is coordinated and steady enough to attempt it alone). Perhaps consider setting up a potty station of books and a few toys that are special for potty time, so your child can be occupied for a few minutes.

Above all, use Praise liberally to build up your child's confidence and sense of becoming the "big kid." Once baby arrives, you should continue this confidence building, but you now have a real live model with which to showcase the mechanics of peeing and pooping. Allow your child to see the baby's dirty diaper from time to time, and watch you change a diaper. You can even enlist your child's help by asking him or her to bring you a clean diaper or hand you the wipes. Use Praise throughout the change, letting your child feel good about the skills she has learned.

As with any big change, it's important for you to carve out some special time with your older child after baby arrives. Whether it's during naptime or on a weekend, treat your big kid with one-on-one activities, such as playing a special game, going out for dessert, or just reading a book together. Using all these techniques, you'll be able to guide your child through the process of becoming an older brother or sister, while still engaging in potty training.

Divorce

A breakup is extremely stressful for all involved, and a child in the midst of potty training could manifest physical symptoms, such as regression, increased accidents, and sometimes outright refusal. Regardless of why the divorce is occurring, it's most common for children of this age to lose confidence and feel uncertain. This should be expected, so if you and your spouse break up, you should agree to put potty training on pause until you can each get a bit settled and provide your child with reliable stability.

However, putting the process on pause most definitely does not mean going backward. It means maintaining current skills and taking a break before moving further. Resist the urge to put your child back into diapers. Although you may find it easier to deal with diapers than with constant potty runs and accidents, you don't want to further erode your child's self-confidence by taking away a success. This could derail the whole potty-training process.

Of utmost importance is remaining on decent terms with your estranged spouse, because ongoing parental conflict can have ramifications well beyond potty training. In fact, conflict can negatively affect your child for the rest of his or her life. Although good relations may not be entirely possible, control your own behaviors and reactions in an effort to keep things civil.

Once you have settled into some semblance of a routine, pick up potty training where you left off. You will probably have to backtrack a bit or progress more slowly than before, but rely on the Role Modeling and Praise strategies to get you back on track. If you've moved, do a couple of Practice Sessions in the new bathroom to give your child a chance to grow familiar with the new surroundings. Keep the potty routine and rules at each home as similar as possible, but they don't need to be exactly the same. Kids can get used to different rules at different places as long as they are consistent in each.

Be on the lookout for common complications, such as regression to an earlier point in the training. For example, a child who was fully pee trained but still learning how to poop on the potty at the time of his parent's divorce may start having frequent daytime wetting accidents. This isn't something to worry too much about in the immediate aftermath of a breakup. Indeed, you really should expect something like this to happen. Reassure your child that you will take care of him, will always be there for him, and will help him through these accidents. Do not punish him for accidents.

Another complication is constipation, which is outlined in the next chapter. When kids feel anxious, they may exert control over the situation by holding in poop. They cannot control the problems between you and your estranged spouse, so they unconsciously seize on the one thing they can control. It's called withholding, and if caught early, can be just a blip on your potty-training radar, but if allowed to take root, it can be an extremely hard habit to break.

This discussion isn't meant to scare you. Divorce is tough enough without throwing in the fear that your child will never make it out of diapers. The truth is that children are extremely resilient. They can handle more than we often give them credit for managing. The key is being mindful in your actions, keeping their point of view in mind and trying to see the big picture of what's best for your child despite your hurt feelings about the breakup. Even though divorce can be difficult, children can make it through resiliently with your help.

•••

While interruptions during the potty-training process may be common, the way you handle them must be specific to your child and the point you have reached in the training process. Remaining calm will help you and your child roll through an interruption without too many problems, particularly if you have a plan for handling the unexpected.

Illness, vacation, and major life changes, such as a move, new baby, or divorce, can impact potty training with the force of a storm. Because children at this age thrive on consistency and routine, an interruption throws them off kilter.

By navigating these situations with an eye on your child's temperament and state of mind, you can restore their balance fairly quickly. If your interruption is a major one, simply maintain the status quo for as long as it takes until your child feels stable again. Sometimes it will make most sense for you to just back off and wait for your child to take the lead and move onto the next step.

10

Overcoming Challenges and Obstacles

Beyond the interruptions discussed in Chapter 9, there may come a time in the potty-training process when you and your child will face a difficult challenge, or even a serious obstacle. Plenty of everyday potty-training hurdles can feel difficult; indeed, potentially every entry on the Skills Acquisition Chart on page 26 can require exertion and be a struggle to achieve. However, as long as your child is moving forward in learning those skills on a fairly regular basis, you can feel confident that your child is getting the hang of it. Remember this is a process and, for most children, it is measured in months not weeks.

If your child seems to be taking longer to learn one of the skills than it took to learn earlier skills, you may be facing the type of problem examined in this chapter. Although this situation may be difficult to pinpoint and measure, if your child is stuck in a rut, you may have hit an obstacle that requires different or more in-depth tactics than outlined in previous chapters. These obstacles can be related to temperament, but they may also be psychological or medical in nature.

In this chapter, you'll learn to identify common challenges and obstacles, as well as ways you can address them with your child. Whether your child is refusing to go in the potty, insisting on a diaper for pooping, or having accidents well past the average age listed on the Skills Acquisition Chart and it's negatively affecting your family life, we'll offer tips and techniques for you to consider. But, first, you need to understand how to keep your own frustration level under control to keep the potty-training process, however long it's taking, on track and moving ahead.

Note: Parents may find some tips and techniques in this chapter that apply to types of common behaviors in the special-needs population. Potty training, after all, is a learned behavior. However, know that special-needs situations are unique and must be addressed individually. If your child has special needs, this chapter may provide helpful information, but it is not a replacement for your family doctor's advice. You might consider reviewing this book with your practitioner for some expert advice that will be specific to your child.

Handling Your Own Frustration

As children approach preschool, and even kindergarten, the pressure to be completely potty trained, dry at night, and accident free grows exponentially. This can increase the frustration that a parent feels and, unfortunately, make the problem worse. But this frustration is real. Nearly all parents experience major frustrations when potty training their children.

We want you to realize that the more frustrated and anxious you become, the more likely it is that your child is going to simply dig in his or her heels, which will make the problem worse. Getting upset or trying to rush or punish your way through an obstacle will only put you on a collision course with your child, and you'll come out farther away from your goal.

No easy trick exists to get you through these challenges. Helping your child overcome any obstacle, including potty training, takes a lot of effort and time. You have to invest in both to shape your child's behavior.

Parent frustration, unfortunately, can also lead to more troublesome problems. It's shocking, but according to the American Academy of Pediatrics, more abuse occurs during toilet training than during any other developmental step. On the AAP.org website, the organization states, "Parents' expectations often exceed the child's abilities or understanding, and the child's frustrations and imperfect attempts at self-control are easily mistaken for willful disobedience."

Of course, this doesn't mean such abuse will happen in your family. We are simply presenting this information to help you better understand this process and to help give you the perspective that this is just one milestone in your child's lifetime. Positive parenting during potty training will set the stage for both you and your child to have a healthy relationship and be better able to handle all those other stressful situations to come.

If you come to a potty-training obstacle you just can't get around and you don't have the time or energy to invest in these tips, it is probably better to back off on training and let things remain the same for a while. Pushing harder, training intermittently, or punishing your child for accidents will just make everything worse. Backing off and going into "idle" mode will do no harm and may just give you or your child enough time to sort things out.

Common Challenges

A few common standouts among the challenges that impede potty training for a large number of children are:

➤ A child will only poop in a diaper or training pants, but not on the potty.
➤ A child refuses to sit on or use the toilet at all.
➤ Daytime wetting.
➤ Nighttime wetting.

We will discuss each of these in this chapter. However, constipation can be a contributor to them all, so we will explore that problem first and give you some tips on how to deal with it.

The Vicious Cycle of Constipation

Constipation is when a child poops less frequently than necessary and has hard, large, and/or painful bowel movements. Many associations exist between constipation and a refusal, or a withholding, of poop. Sometimes this manifests itself as a child who goes off by himself to do it in his diaper, one who is potty trained but demands a diaper to poop in, or a child who literally holds it until he cannot control it any longer.

It seems that early pain experiences with poop can lead some children to become constipated. The child associates pain with using the potty, and this leads to a vicious cycle of avoiding the pain by holding in the poop, which only causes additional constipation and pain. So, the cycle starts all over again. Even an infant who experiences pain while pooping can learn to withhold poop and become constipated. Often, a constipated child has a difficult time getting the poop out even when he or she is trying. This contributes even more to the pain and avoidance, thereby making the problem worse. Children who have been constipated before are more likely to become so again. Constipation is fairly common during the potty-training stage of life, but can also become an issue when a child starts school.

Typically, children older than two years of age have one or two normal bowel movements per day, but fewer can still be considered normal. If you've tracked your child's schedule and know that he usually poops once a day and now he hasn't gone for two days, he may be experiencing constipation. However, if his normal schedule is once every two days and he isn't experiencing any discomfort, then there most likely isn't anything to worry about.

Sometimes, children who are constipated engage in behavior that we might consider strange or frustrating, such as hiding in a corner or behind furniture to poop, squatting or contorting themselves into unusual positions, or arching their backs and stiffening their legs. It may even look like the "potty dance" of going up on their tiptoes or wriggling around. In some cases, this may even appear comical, but it is anything but that. Instead of trying to poop by doing these things, they are really trying to hold their poop in because they are frightened, worried, or perhaps embarrassed. Soiling or streaking in their underwear can also be a sign of constipation, as can increased wetting accidents, as a child tries but fails to control his bodily functions in all toileting areas.

If you suspect your child is constipated, contact your child's primary care provider. Depending on the time frame and symptoms, the doctor may suggest changes in your child's diet, such as adding a cup of prune, pear, or apple juice (100 percent fruit) or adding foods with higher amounts of fiber, such as broccoli, spinach, apricots, sweet potatoes, and whole-grain bread. Reducing your child's intake of other foods, particularly dairy products, such as cow's milk, cheese, yogurt and ice cream, may also help. Sometimes, your doctor may recommend an over-the-counter remedy, such as a fiber supplement, many of which can be stirred into juice and even frozen into popsicles that make them more palatable to your child.

If constipation is a recurring situation, your doctor may want to examine your child and determine if there is a root cause beyond diet that is contributing to it. Sometimes, doctors prescribe medicinal laxatives, suppositories, or enemas. Constipation, if left unchecked, can cause other medical problems, so it does need to be addressed right away. If you can catch and treat it early, it's less apt to become a recurring problem.

Super Duper Diaper Pooper

Your child has got peeing in the potty down pat—and may even be an expert at that! But when it comes to pooping, it seems as if he's not potty trained at all. If he's in underwear already, he may even verbally demand a diaper or a pull-up to poop in. It so happens that many children fall into the category of super duper diaper pooper. While this is a tongue-in-cheek reference that hopefully puts a smile on your face, this behavior can be extraordinarily frustrating to a parent.

But there is some good news. The first is that if your child is doing that well with her peeing skills and is not already in underwear, she's ready for that step. Second, if your child is asking or demanding a diaper to poop in, she's recognizing the urge to poop and acting on that feeling. Thus, you can cross off two more skills on the Skills Acquisition Chart!

At this point, however, you do need to investigate why your child doesn't want to poop in the potty, particularly because this behavior is one of the top causes of constipation. And, you want to avoid constipation at all possible. A refusal to poop in the potty is likely a sensory issue that centers on the water in the bowl splashing up, the smells associated with pooping, or fear that a part of the body is going to get flushed. Although these are common fears, we also need to return to the idea presented at the beginning of this book. From when he was a baby, your child's been under the belief that pooping in the diaper is the right thing to do, whether he really thought about it or not. Pooping in a diaper is all he's known; it's what he's comfortable doing. So, for your child, this is a huge change, and you need to keep this perspective in mind as your child develops.

Outright Refusing the Potty

Another common challenge is when a child refuses to use the potty or toilet entirely. She doesn't want anything to do with it whatsoever. Perhaps she started potty training just fine, but then one day changed her mind and decided this potty thing just wasn't for her. This is really not willful disobedience; she's not trying to be frustrating.

You'll need to do a little investigating to see figure out the cause of this behavior, but it's possibly the result of a combination of factors. You may simply have to go back to some of the basics of potty training. Give her some time and then work your way back to where you were in the process before the refusal started.

Revisit the temperament quiz in Chapter 1 because her personality may have developed since you first took the quiz. Remember, a secondary or even tertiary temperament can play a big role in potty training. In particular, Impulsive and Strong-Willed Children will refuse if they feel pushed into training before they are ready. Discuss the issue with any child-care providers or family members. Specifically ask if any recent incidents which may be contributing to the refusal.

Increased independence as your child gets older may also trigger some defiance, which may manifest itself in a refusal to use the potty. If you think this is the case, be sure to involve him in the clean-up as a natural consequence of the accident, but do not blame or shame him.

Consider his personal comfort issues. If you started him on the toilet, perhaps he's feeling unstable way up there, so consider getting a step stool or a small potty chair. Even if his temperament didn't score into the Sensory-Oriented group, it may be that there is some sensitivity to the smells, sounds, and textures in the bathroom.

Think about her fears. Possibly an old fear is rearing its ugly head again or maybe she's developed new ones. If she seems to panic about the idea of going into the bathroom or sitting on the toilet, it may be that she's more scared than stubborn.

If you haven't tried Nakedtime yet, now might be a good time to test it out. There's no potty involved, at least at first, and it could just be the thing to spur him or her toward the toilet.

Thought through it all and still can't figure it out? Take a deep breath and sift through it all again. It's most likely that your child is refusing because she's either not ready, on sensory-overload, or scared of something. Sometimes just backing off is enough to do the trick.

Talk with your pediatrician. The doctor can rule out any medical issues that might be causing the refusal, and also ask your child some questions that might elicit an answer.

Note: If your child is under three years of age and you're just starting potty training in earnest, his refusal is most likely a sign that he isn't ready to train. Back off the active potty-training techniques and work instead on the Universal Strategies that don't require him to do anything. Communicate clearly, be a potty role model, and keep a log of his elimination schedule. Give him some time and then be ready to start when he is ready to learn.

Daytime Wetting

Every child has accidents during potty training, and even having a *lot* of accidents is very common. This is a natural part of the potty-training process, and we urge you to carefully consider your reactions to these accidents. As already stated, a matter-of-fact response that is age appropriate will be your best bet.

Impulsive Children, in particular, are vulnerable to increased daytime wetting. Children with this temperament tend not to notice their body's signals, wait too long, and have a hard time stopping whatever activity they are involved in at the time to go to the bathroom. Potty training is boring to Impulsive Children and going in a diaper is the easier, and thus preferred, method of elimination.

Whether or not your answers to the quiz in Chapter 1 placed your child into the Impulsive Child category, daytime wetting is a problem that can be dealt with in a number of ways. First, understand your child's attitude toward wetting. Is he uncaring or oblivious? Does she act defensive or sensitive and embarrassed about the accidents? Is he truly trying and devastated each time he wets? Your tactics will obviously need to be based on the attitude of your child, so carefully consider these questions.

The use of very absorbent diapers or training pants could be caus-ing a lack of awareness—he simply doesn't feel the pee until it's too late. Consider switching to a less absorbent product or going straight to un-derwear so that he can feel when he's wet. Trying Nakedtime can help in these instances, too, as your child will have a clear view of what's happen-ing down there and should notice it. It certainly is messier, but some-times there's no way around the mess: think of it as a teaching tool. What you want is to increase your child's awareness of the wetness. Any potty-training child must be aware of the urge to pee while enough time is left to make it to the potty. Sometimes you have to backtrack a little bit to reinforce the association in your child's mind between that urge and the actual act of peeing or pooping.

Cueing a child who is a daytime wetter is really important. Imple-ment a Hop on the Pot schedule and use Coaching techniques to tell her exactly what you want her to do and when. Use Praise liberally, and make sure you're focused on what she's doing right and not what she's doing wrong.

Sometimes a child who has a great many accidents during the day is simply engrossed in another activity and doesn't want to stop for a potty break. Playing with friends, watching television, building a block tower, anything that captures their attention and imagination is going to take priority. With these kids, it can be extremely important in terms of their motivation for potty training to make sure they can go back to that fun activity after they try to go potty. This is a powerful reward and will reinforce the behavior of trying.

For example, if your child's play activity is interrupted in order to go to the bathroom, a negative association is created in their brain: going to the potty equals the end of my fun. To top it off, there's a good chance that in the commotion of going to the potty, you both get distracted or you see this as a natural time to transition to something else, such as a nap or a meal. Resist doing that and be very deliberate about making sure your child returns to the favored activity after using the potty. This will rein-force the idea that the activity is simply put on pause, and it is not going to stop because of going to the potty. If you do happen to be close to a tran-sition time, try to delay your schedule for at least 10 minutes so that you clear the negative association between potty and stopping the fun activity.

It's not common, but there are sometimes medical reasons for daytime wetting. If you are concerned about this or it's become an ongoing issue beyond the time frame you'd expect, give your child's primary care provider a call. Pediatricians can evaluate a child to make sure that no medical issue is contributing to the problem. If they do find something, they can discuss available treatment options with you.

Nighttime Wetting

As outlined in the Skills Acquisition Chart on page 26, waking up dry in the morning is one of the last skills your child will learn. It may take a very long time for your child to be able to unconsciously control his or her bladder muscles during sleep. Generally, children are considered potty trained, even if they are continuing to have a problem with nighttime wetting, but that doesn't make it any easier for your child or for you. Hopefully this statistic will allay your concerns a bit. The American Academy of Pediatrics estimates that 20 percent of 5-year-olds, 10 percent of 7-year-olds, and 5 percent of 10-year-olds may still wet the bed. In most cases, as a child's body grows and matures, the bedwetting problem resolves itself.

Sometimes nighttime bedwetting is an inherited trait, as it's been known to run in families. While this has more to do with genetics than with anything you can address through potty training, how you handle these accidents should help the process and protect your child's self-esteem.

Regardless of the reasons, make sure your child understands there is no shame. Explain that many other kids his age still have accidents at night. Don't allow siblings or other family members to ridicule your child, as this will not fix the problem. Use layering to keep his bed clean and dry, as described on page 74, which will also help make clean-ups in the middle of the night easier. Waking your child after a few hours of sleep to go to the bathroom can help to train his bladder, but you need to make sure he is fully awake so he starts to learn to get up on his own. Limiting liquids before bedtime may also help reduce accidents, but if your concern is that the bedwetting has continued past his fifth birthday, there are usually medical or biological reasons for the accidents that have nothing to do with how much he has to drink.

Alarm systems are an option, but discuss this approach with your child's doctor before trying these products. Alarms make a sound if they sense any wetness, thereby giving your child a cue that she needs to get up and go to the bathroom. While some urine is usually already on the sheets, she can finish urinating in the toilet or just try. Eventually, this can train her to associate the urge to go and holding it until she can get to the bathroom. Additionally, an alarm is a form of negative reinforcement, so if your child wants to avoid the disruption of the alarm and subsequent middle of the night activity associated with the accident, she will, over time, start to control her bladder more successfully.

Ways to Use Universal Strategies to Address Problems

In addition to the above suggestions, we'll call out a few of the Universal Strategies from Chapter 3 as particularly helpful in facing these challenges. A good idea is to re-read that chapter and think about whether any of the other strategies might resonate with your child and his or her specific problem.

Increase Practice Sessions

Particularly if you've caught the constipation problem early, before withholding the poop has become a habit for your child, you can strategically schedule some practice sessions specifically for pooping. Choose a time when your child is more apt to need to poop, either based on your tracking her schedule or on waiting 5 to 30 minutes after a meal. These sessions should be pleasant and motivating. You could allow her to have a special toy only during these practice sessions or perhaps read a favorite book during this time.

However, don't overdo these motivators, especially if your child is annoyed by practice sessions. One or two special things are enough. Stay with your child; don't leave her alone in the bathroom during these practice sessions. If she's using a potty chair, perhaps you can sit on the toilet next to her and role model at the same time. If she's sitting on the toilet, get her a step stool or something on which to brace her feet, so she will feel more stable and give her leverage as she learns to move her bowels.

Keep the atmosphere positive; practice sessions are not punishment! This is an important message to convey because she's already starting to associate pooping with negativity, discomfort, or pain. To remind her of that negativity will only hinder the process further.

Reward Positive Behavior and Give Good Directions

These two Universal Strategies go hand in hand and work especially well together when facing an obstacle. Start wherever your child is in terms of pooping, and then work to shape that behavior by directing a sequence of behaviors and rewards, each of which moves the child a little closer to the final goal of pooping in the potty.

Let's say your child is demanding a diaper and then going to poop in the corner, refusing to even go into the bathroom. Start by simply rewarding him for telling you that he pooped or even just for the act of pooping. The idea is to get him to relax about going poop in general. The more we try to push him, the less relaxed he will be, and it's hard for a child to poop when he's not relaxed. You are shaping his behavior by getting him to poop with regularity in a relaxed manner as the first step.

The second step, which should follow fairly quickly, is to tell your child that she's allowed to use the diaper to poop and it's okay to want to go off by herself, but she must do it in the bathroom. You can entice her there with some favorite music or other incentive will make it more pleasant for her. If you have more than one bathroom, let her choose which one to use. Reward her each time she poops while she's in the bathroom. If she poops in another location, congratulate her for pooping, but do not give the reward unless she does it in the bathroom. Can you see how you're starting to shape her behavior in the right direction?

Next, follow up with directions to sit on the potty or toilet with the lid closed while pooping into the diaper. Again, stay positive about the whole process but only reward that specific behavior. Then, he can keep the diaper on but needs to be sitting on the potty or toilet with the lid open. Finally, potty lid open, diaper off, and then some bigger reward for this final step!

It is important that parents reward each step along the way. You can break down this process in any way that works for your child, as long as the last step is the final goal. If you find your child is having a hard time being in the bathroom at first, break that behavior down even further and insert a step where the child is in the hallway near the bathroom before you try to get him or her inside.

Rewarding the small steps along the way instead of just the final outcome can help your child maintain her motivation. Small successes can be very motivating, whereas a single big incentive for the final goal that the child can never seem to reach may be very defeating. Indeed, any behavior you want your child to learn can be broken down into a series of steps that shape the behavior by rewarding closer and closer approximations of it. Your child will not only learn the final behavior, but will also absorb the idea of working hard toward a goal, which is a valuable lesson.

Up the Ante with Rewards

When we described the Universal Strategy of Offering Positive Reinforcement or rewards, it was probably pretty obvious that we prefer to recommend social reinforcers, such as praise, high-fives, and special outings. These types of rewards work very well with most children during the potty-training process and have the added benefit of teaching children persistence, tolerance, patience, bravery, and commitment to a goal.

However, when dealing with tough challenges and obstacles, such as refusal or withholding, over which your child has ultimate control, it's okay to up the ante with more tangible rewards. The possibility that prizes will really inspire your child to do something he or she doesn't want to do is worth a try, particularly if it gets you out of an intractable situation in potty training. In most cases, it's better to resolve the problem more quickly with prizes than let it drag out and potentially cause more problems later on, not the least of which are medical ramifications of behaviors like withholding poop. One caveat to this advice is you cannot offer prizes to solve a problem over which your child has no control, like nighttime wetting. That will not help the process and will only frustrate you both.

Why not just start with these bigger ticket rewards in the first place? Well, many children won't need it. Praise and other social motivators are often enough to spur the behavior you want to see, and tangible rewards may actually inhibit development of internal motivation. In the short term, when used to overcome a specific problem, such rewards shouldn't result in any lasting negative effects, and they may be just the push you need to get over whatever hurdle you're facing. It's a compromise that is worth it when you've already tried everything else.

Present the reward in a purposeful, deliberate, and strategic manner. Use the *if/then* and *after/then* contingency explained in the Universal Strategy of Giving Good Directions in Chapter 3. Additionally, communicate to your child that the biggest rewards come when your expectations for a pattern of behavior are met. This will prevent the child from thinking that he can do what you are asking once, claim the prize, and then go back to his old habits.

Potty Talk

Dad: After you try to go potty, we can play that game you wanted to play! (cars, dolls, LEGOS, whatever he or she likes best)

Mom: After you go poop in the potty for a whole week, not even once in your diaper, we'll go down to the store and you can pick out that toy you really want!

Layer in smaller rewards for individual steps to help shape his behavior, with the most valuable prize awarded for reaching the final goal. You can create a potty chart so your child can actually see her progress toward the final reward. You could make it a sort of "reward menu" to give your child options in terms of what he would like to earn with his behavior. For young children, a picture menu or perhaps a set of cards with icons would be a good idea. You can download some potty charts from our website, www.stressfreeparent.com. A chart gives him a sense of control in the process, as he gets to choose what he would like to earn and is then invested in the endeavor. Those types of rewards will be different for every child, so asking him or her directly will ensure you don't pick something that's not very motivating.

Punishments

When dealing with potty-training problems, scolding, negative consequences, or punishment of any kind should be avoided. You need to know that you're not going to punish your child into better potty behavior. Especially during these early years, lengthy discussions or lectures about proper potty use are not going to be effective and may, in fact, inhibit the child because he will start to associate the negativity of those lectures with using the potty. This has the opposite effect of what you intended with the punishments. Instead of spurring your child to do better, you're reinforcing the negatives and actually encouraging more problems.

Especially when it comes to fears, sensitivities and nighttime accidents—those things your child has no control over—punishments can severely impact her self-esteem, which can have long-lasting ramifications. These early years are crucial to developing her sense of self-worth and self-confidence, and you need to safeguard those feelings in your child. Remember to Keep Perspective. This is but one of many milestones in her life, and she will cross the finish line of potty training. Just like any goal, it takes some people longer to reach it than others.

When to Seek Professional Help

There are rare times when a parent encounters potty behaviors in their child that require professional intervention. When things aren't going the way you think they should or if you have concerns, the first person you should consult is your child's pediatrician. It's probably a good idea to alert the doctor when you are planning to start potty training, so that she/he can keep an eye out for any related medical issues. If yours is a special needs or developmentally delayed child, a pediatrician will be able to more specifically advise you when to start potty training and how best to proceed.

This book cannot begin to address every conceivable situation, and your doctor is where you should go to get advice particular to your child's physical, social, and emotional well-being. This chapter should not be used as a substitute for a more in-depth investigation of causes of problems and possible treatments.

Some cases in which a pediatrician may refer you to another doctor include:

- A child who is using toileting as a way to express anger or aggression.
- Parents who are trapped in a power struggle over potty training and don't know where to turn next.
- Parents who are having trouble keeping their own frustrations about the process in check.
- Severe or sudden regression in potty training that seems unrelated to anything the parent knows about in the child's life.
- Physical problems, such as constipation or pain when pooping or peeing.
- Emotional issues, such as withholding.

Your pediatrician or family doctor is the best first line of defense for potty-training problems, but also the gatekeeper for additional intervention, so keep them apprised of your plans and progress.

•••

Challenges and obstacles during potty training can interfere not only with the process, but also with your entire life. They are frustrating and even maddening at times. From our adult perspective, these skills don't seem so hard to learn. But if you look at the situation from your child's perspective, you may see these challenges and obstacles more clearly and thus be able to handle them more successfully.

Dealing with your own frustrations is really crucial, so work to maintain your composure. The more anxious or angry you become, the more likely it is that the problem will get worse. Using positive parenting techniques will contribute to a healthy relationship with your child and pay dividends in the future.

The types of challenges and obstacles outlined in this chapter hit many families hard. The most common challenge we hear from parents is that their child will only poop in a diaper or training pants, but not on the potty. Other children refuse to sit on or use the toilet at all. Still others have protracted daytime and/or nighttime wetting accidents that can sabotage their self-esteem. Some will experience constipation, which can erupt into a vicious cycle if not checked.

Handle these using the Universal Strategies and advanced techniques outlined in this chapter, Chapter 3, and your child's temperament-specific chapter. In some cases, it may make sense for you to take the temperament quiz again, because a latent personality trait may have started to emerge in your child. Addressing it with special potty-training techniques will help you move forward.

Above all, remember that this is just your child's first big developmental milestone in a long list of them to come. Your child will not go to college in diapers, despite the fact that, right now, it feels as if she will.

Conclusion

Potty training is not really a complex time in your child's life, once you're done with it. Before you start, however, it can seem daunting. Our aim with this book is to give you a vast array of tools to put in your parenting arsenal, some clues as to which will resonate best with your particular child, and then plenty of backup ideas just in case.

We hope you've learned some information from the examination of your child's personality and his or her main motivations and common reactions. Being the thoughtful, caring parent, you are trying to view this change of life from your child's perspective. And a big change it is, for you both, really. Becoming potty trained will open up a whole new world; it's exciting and gratifying to see your child safely through this milestone. Regardless of whether yours is a Goal-Directed, Sensory-Oriented, Internalizing, Impulsive, or Strong-Willed Child, let them progress at their own pace, find what works best to positively reinforce their behavior, and make sure to praise them for their efforts.

nderstand that your Internalizer may need some
e of trust enough to include the potty. You see
-Willed Daughter's attempts to control the sit-
. on the potty at all until after you'd dropped the
whole weeks. Then she sat and went—her pride intact
ladder regulated. You have more insight into your Sensory-
ented Son's extreme reactions to accidents and can help him successfully work through it. You are considering using nakedtime to more clearly
direct your Impulsive Child's boundless energy toward correct toileting
habits. And you now have your Goal-Directed Child going gangbusters
on the potty because you capitalized on her interest in wearing big-girl
undies like her cousin.

Beyond toilet training, we hope you'll take the broad strokes of the
picture we've painted of your child's temperament and allow them to
color your parenting techniques with other challenging situations. Between now and the age of five, your daughter or son will be faced with
a thousand more learning processes whereby they cannot specifically
articulate what they need from you. Our insights into the way your child's
mind works should help you address these needs, if you can step back
from the emotional aspects for a moment and consider his or her character traits.

Make the most of what you've learned to benefit your child but
also learn from the experience of having potty trained your unique child,
and incorporate both the successes and failures into your way of thinking. Let that information guide your future parenting experiences. Fine-
tune your tactics and subtly integrate the lessons of potty training to help
you become a better problem solver and advocate for your child.

As they grow and mature, she/he will be better able to adapt and
manage tricky situations, even learning huge new skills, without so much
hands-on assistance from you. But you will still understand what causes
them anxiety, aggravation, or anger. When they're older, they'll be able
to learn some of these life lessons for themselves, and your understanding
will help to guide them along the right path.

Say, for example, your daughter comes home from third grade one
day crying and won't tell you why. Remembering her tendency to Internalize matters, you may give her some time to calm down and process her

experience, and then go to her and ask whether she wants to bounce some solutions to her problem off you. Understanding her inclination to consider all negative possibilities before determining her course of action, you've just offered her the one thing she can't get anywhere else—a safe place to express her fears. Perhaps you'll offer to role play her response to a friend's harsh comment and she'll be able to go back to school the next day feeling confident about herself.

Or, perhaps your Strong-Willed Son is fuming after football practice because his coach was yelling and telling him he wasn't running the right play. As a small child, you were attuned to his every mood swing and adapted your reaction based on his. But as he matures, you know he's going to have to learn how to deal with situations like this, and others that are much worse, on his own. So, you don't intervene. You allow him to simmer down on his own and then explain that he's going to have to find a way to deal with the coach's temper. You might, if the timing is right, point out that the coach sounds like he's also a Strong-Willed personality type, and that the two of them need to get in alignment for everything to work out.

As long as your child is not being pushed over the edge emotionally, helping them process situations like this will make them stronger people and better able to deal with all that life throws at them. You can learn a great deal more about these types of situations and how to shape behavior in our latest book in the Stress-Free Parent series: *Stress-Free Discipline*.

As we've said throughout this book, a parent's job is to facilitate and manage, but your child is his or her own person now, ready to potty train and enter a whole new world of independence.

Congratulations!

Index